# TEACHER'S PET PUBLICATIONS

## LITPLAN TEACHER PACK
for
The Call of the Wild
based on the book by
Jack London

Written by
Mary B. Collins

© 1996 Teacher's Pet Publications
All Rights Reserved

ISBN 978-1-60249-138-0
Ite No. 304940

This **LitPlan** for Jack London's
*Call of the Wild*
has been brought to you by Teacher's Pet Publications, Inc.

Copyright Teacher's Pet Publications 1996

Only the student materials in this unit plan (such as worksheets, study questions, and tests) may be reproduced multiple times for use in the purchaser's classroom.

For any additional copyright questions,
contact Teacher's Pet Publications.

www.tpet.com

# TABLE OF CONTENTS - *The Call of the Wild*

| | |
|---|---|
| Introduction | 5 |
| Unit Objectives | 7 |
| Reading Assignment Sheet | 8 |
| Unit Outline | 9 |
| Study Questions (Short Answer) | 13 |
| Quiz/Study Questions (Multiple Choice) | 19 |
| Pre-reading Vocabulary Worksheets | 31 |
| Lesson One (Introductory Lesson) | 41 |
| Nonfiction Assignment Sheet | 43 |
| Oral Reading Evaluation Form | 45 |
| Writing Assignment 1 | 52 |
| Writing Assignment 2 | 55 |
| Writing Assignment 3 | 62 |
| Writing Evaluation Form | 60 |
| Vocabulary Review Activities | 53 |
| Extra Writing Assignments/Discussion ?s | 49 |
| Unit Review Activities | 64 |
| Unit Tests | 67 |
| Unit Resource Materials | 93 |
| Vocabulary Resource Materials | 113 |

# A FEW NOTES ABOUT THE AUTHOR
# JACK LONDON

LONDON, Jack (1876-1916). The novelist and short-story writer Jack London was, in his lifetime, one of the most popular authors in the world. After World War I his fame was eclipsed in the United States by a new generation of writers, but he remained popular in many other countries, especially in the Soviet Union, for his romantic tales of adventure and survival.

John Griffith London was born in San Francisco on Jan. 12, 1876. His family was poor, and he was forced to go to work early in life to support himself. At 17 he sailed to Japan and Siberia on a seal-hunting voyage. He was largely self-taught, reading voluminously in libraries and spending a year at the University of California. In the late 1890s he joined the gold rush to the Klondike. This experience gave him material for his first book, 'The Son of Wolf', published in 1900, and for 'Call of the Wild' (1903), one of his most popular stories.

In his writing career of 17 years, London produced 50 books and many short stories. He wrote mostly for money, to meet ever-increasing expenses. His fame as a writer gave him a ready audience as a spokesman for a peculiar and inconsistent blend of socialism and racial superiority.

London's works, all hastily written, are of uneven quality. The best books are the Klondike tales, which also include 'White Fang' (1906) and 'Burning Daylight' (1910). His most enduring novel is probably the autobiographical 'Martin Eden' (1909), but the exciting 'Sea Wolf' (1904) continues to have great appeal for young readers.

In 1910 London settled near Glen Ellen, Calif., where he intended to build his dream home, "Wolf House." After the house burned down before completion in 1913, he was a broken and sick man. His death on Nov. 22, 1916, from an overdose of drugs, was probably a suicide.

--- Courtesy of Compton's Learning Company

# INTRODUCTION

This unit has been designed to develop students' reading, writing, thinking, and language skills through exercises and activities related to *The Call of the Wild* by Jack London. It includes eighteen lessons, supported by extra resource materials.

The **introductory lesson** introduces students to one main theme of the novel by having a guest speaker come in to speak to the class about the role of wild animals in our world. Students are also given the materials they will be using during the unit. At the end of the lesson, students begin the pre-reading work for the first reading assignment.

The **reading assignments** are approximately thirty pages each; some are a little shorter while others are a little longer. Students have approximately 15 minutes of pre-reading work to do prior to each reading assignment. This pre-reading work involves reviewing the study questions for the assignment and doing some vocabulary work for 8 to 10 vocabulary words they will encounter in their reading.

The **study guide questions** are fact-based questions; students can find the answers to these questions right in the text. These questions come in two formats: short answer or multiple choice. The best use of these materials is probably to use the short answer version of the questions as study guides for students (since answers will be more complete), and to use the multiple choice version for occasional quizzes. If your school has the appropriate machinery, it might be a good idea to make transparencies of your answer keys for the overhead projector.

The **vocabulary work** is intended to enrich students' vocabularies as well as to aid in the students' understanding of the book. Prior to each reading assignment, students will complete a two-part worksheet for approximately 8 to 10 vocabulary words in the upcoming reading assignment. Part I focuses on students' use of general knowledge and contextual clues by giving the sentence in which the word appears in the text. Students are then to write down what they think the words mean based on the words' usage. Part II nails down the definitions of the words by giving students dictionary definitions of the words and having students match the words to the correct definitions based on the words' contextual usage. Students should then have an understanding of the words when they meet them in the text.

After the reading assignments, students will go back and formulate answers for the study guide questions. Discussion of these questions serves as a **review** of the most important events and ideas presented in the reading assignments.

After students have read the novel and have an understanding of the literal level, a lesson is devoted to the **extra discussion questions/writing assignments**. These questions focus on interpretation, critical analysis and personal response, employing a variety of thinking skills and adding to the students' understanding of the novel.

There is also a **vocabulary review** lesson which pulls together all of the fragmented vocabulary lists for the reading assignments and gives students a review of all of the words they have studied.

There are three **writing assignments** in this unit, each with the purpose of informing, persuading, or having students express personal opinions. The first assignment is for personal opinions: students write their opinions about the relationship(s) between people and animals on our planet. The second assignment is to inform: students choose an animal on the endangered species list, do background research, and write a report explaining the background, giving the current status of the animal, and making recommendations for appropriate actions that can be taken to help the animal. The third assignment is to persuade and to give students a chance to be creative: students create a mail-out piece for the National Wildlife Foundation (or any wilderness/conservation association) to persuade people to make a contribution.

There is a **nonfiction reading assignment** related to Writing Assignment 2 mentioned above. During one class period, students also make **oral presentations** about the nonfiction pieces they have read. This not only exposes all students to a wealth of information, it also gives students the opportunity to practice **public speaking**.

One class period is devoted to discussion of survival and camping techniques. The **group activity** which follows the discussion has students working in small groups to actually plan a camping trip.

The **review lesson** pulls together all of the aspects of the unit. The teacher is given four or five choices of activities or games to use which all serve the same basic function of reviewing all of the information presented in the unit.

The **unit test** comes in two formats: multiple choice-matching-true/false or short answer. As a convenience, two different tests for each format have been included. In addition there is an Advanced Short Answer Unit Test for students who need more of a challenge.

There are additional **support materials** included with this unit. The **extra activities section** includes suggestions for an in-class library, crossword and word search puzzles related to the novel, and extra vocabulary worksheets. There is a list of **bulletin board ideas** which gives the teacher suggestions for bulletin boards to go along with this unit. In addition, there is a list of **extra class activities** the teacher could choose from to enhance the unit or as a substitution for an exercise the teacher might feel is inappropriate for his/her class. The **teacher's manual** has the answer keys for the worksheets, tests, puzzles, etc. The **student packet** has worksheets, tests, puzzles, etc. left blank for students to fill-in. Materials in the student packet may be reproduced for use in the teacher's classroom without infringement of copyrights. Teachers' manuals may not be reproduced without the written consent of Teacher's Pet Publications, Inc.

# UNIT OBJECTIVES - *The Call of the Wild*

1. Through reading London's *Call of the Wild*, students will study the importance of adapting to the changes in one's life and environment.

2. Students will demonstrate their understanding of the text on four levels: factual, interpretive, critical and personal.

3. Students will discuss the theme of survival of the fittest.

4. Students will discuss the importance of wilderness and animals in our world.

5. Students will discuss survival skills and actually plan a camping trip.

6. Students will be given the opportunity to practice reading aloud and silently to improve their skills in each area.

7. Students will answer questions to demonstrate their knowledge and understanding of the main events and characters in *The Call of the Wild* as they relate to the author's theme development.

8. Students will enrich their vocabularies and improve their understanding of the novel through the vocabulary lessons prepared for use in conjunction with the novel.

9. The writing assignments in this unit are geared to several purposes:
    a. To have students demonstrate their abilities to inform, to persuade, or to express their own personal ideas
    Note: Students will demonstrate ability to write effectively to <u>inform</u> by developing and organizing facts to convey information. Students will demonstrate the ability to write effectively to <u>persuade</u> by selecting and organizing relevant information, establishing an argumentative purpose, and by designing an appropriate strategy for an identified audience. Students will demonstrate the ability to write effectively to <u>express personal ideas</u> by selecting a form and its appropriate elements.
    b. To check the students' reading comprehension
    c. To make students think about the ideas presented by the novel
    d. To encourage logical thinking
    e. To provide an opportunity to practice good grammar and improve students' use of the English language.

10. Students will read aloud, report, and participate in large and small group discussions to improve their public speaking and personal interaction skills.

## READING ASSIGNMENT SHEET - *The Call of the Wild*

| Date Assigned | Reading Assignment | Completion Date |
|---|---|---|
|  | Part I |  |
|  | Part II |  |
|  | Part III |  |
|  | Part IV |  |
|  | Part V |  |
|  | Part VI |  |
|  | Part VII |  |

## UNIT OUTLINE - *The Call of the Wild*

| 1<br>Introduction<br><br>PV Part I | 2<br><br>Read Part I | 3<br><br>PVR Parts II-IV | 4<br>Quiz/?s I-IV<br><br>PVR Part V | 5<br><br>PVR Parts VI-VII |
|---|---|---|---|---|
| 6<br>Study ?s V-VII<br><br>Assign Extra ?s | 7<br><br>Discussion | 8<br><br>Writing Assignment 1 | 9<br><br>Vocabulary | 10<br><br>Library<br><br>Nonfiction Assignment |
| 11<br><br>Writing Assignment 2 | 12<br><br>Nonfiction Reports | 13<br><br>Speaker | 14<br><br>Trip Plans | 15<br><br>Trip Plans |
| 16<br><br>Writing Assignment 3 | 17<br><br>Review | 18<br><br>Test | | |

Key: P = Preview Study Questions  V = Vocabulary Work  R = Read

# STUDY GUIDE QUESTIONS

## SHORT ANSWER STUDY GUIDE QUESTIONS - *The Call of the Wild*

Part I
1. Where did Buck live? What was his life like there?
2. What events were taking place elsewhere which would affect Buck's life?
3. Who was Manuel?
4. What did Manuel do to Buck?
5. Identify "the man in the red sweater."

Part II
1. What happened to Curly?
2. What did Buck learn from seeing Curly so swiftly killed?
3. What did "ho" and "mush" mean?
4. Identify Spitz.
5. How did the dogs sleep at night?
6. How did Perrault honor Buck?
7. How has Buck changed in Part II as compared to the way he was at the beginning of the story in Part I?
8. What did the dog-driver do for Buck?

Part III
1. Why did Buck and Spitz first fight?
2. What unexpected incident kept Buck and Spitz from finishing their first fight?
3. What happened to the team after Buck "stood up" to Spitz?
4. What caused the final battle between Buck and Spitz?
5. What was the outcome of the final battle between Spitz and Buck?

Part IV
1. How did Buck become lead dog?
2. Was Buck a good lead dog?
3. Why did Francois and Perrault give up the team of dogs?
4. In what condition were the dogs when they pulled into Dawson?

Part V
1. Identify Charles and Hal.
2. Who was Mercedes?
3. Why couldn't the dogs move the sled?
4. Describe Hal, Charles and Mercedes.
5. What happened to all but the five experienced dogs?
6. How did Buck meet John Thornton?
7. What happened to Charles, Hal, Mercedes, and the sled team?

*Call of the Wild* Short Answer Study Questions Page 2

Part VI
1. Identify Skeet and Nig.
2. How was Buck's life with John Thornton different from his life with his other masters?
3. How did Buck react to Hans and Pete?
4. Why did Buck attack "Black" Burton?
5. How did Buck save John Thornton?
6. What extraordinary feat did Buck do out of love for John?

Part VII
1. How much money did John Thornton win on his bet, and what did he do with it?
2. To where do Buck and John travel?
3. How does Buck respond to his trip into the wilderness?
4. How did Buck kill the moose?
5. What happened to John Thornton?
6. What did Buck do to the Indians who killed his master?
7. With his master slain and all ties to mankind broken, what does Buck do?

# ANSWER KEY SHORT ANSWER STUDY GUIDE QUESTIONS
## *The Call of the Wild*

Part I

1. Where did Buck live? What was his life like there?
    He lived in the Santa Clara Valley in California where he was well-treated, well-fed, and had no work. He led a life of leisure.

2. What events were taking place elsewhere which would affect Buck's life?
    People had found gold in the north, and they needed good dogs to pull sleds.

3. Who was Manuel?
    He was a gardener's helper for Judge Miller, Buck's owner.

4. What did Manuel do to Buck?
    He stole Buck and sold him for profit.

5. Identify "the man in the red sweater."
    The man in the red sweater teaches Buck the law of the club, that a man with a club is someone to obey.

Part II

1. What happened to Curly?
    Curly was attacked and killed by the other dogs.

2. What did Buck learn from seeing Curly so swiftly killed?
    He learned that there was no "fair" play here. Once you were down, that would be the end of you. He decided then and there that he would never go down.

3. What did "ho" and "mush" mean?
    "Ho" meant "stop"; "mush" meant "go."

4. Identify Spitz.
    Spitz killed Curly and became Buck's enemy. He is a vicious, wolf-like dog that often hurts the other dogs.

5. How did the dogs sleep at night?
    They dug holes in the snow and slept in there, using the snow as insulation to maintain their body heat.

6. How did Perrault honor Buck?
    He carefully examined Buck's feet at the end of the day.

7. How has Buck changed in Part II as compared to the way he was at the beginning of the story in Part I?
    Buck is becoming wise to the ways of the wild. He has had to give up his life of leisure to learn how to work and fight for his own survival.

8. What did the dog-driver do for Buck?
    He made moccasins for Buck's feet out of his own shoe leather.

Part III

1. Why did Buck and Spitz first fight?
    Spitz stole Buck's sleeping hole.

2. What unexpected incident kept Buck and Spitz from finishing their first fight?
    Some huskies raided the camp for food. The dogs fought to defend their food and camp against the intruders.

3. What happened to the team after Buck "stood up" to Spitz?
    A general mutiny took place, and the team no longer worked together.

4. What caused the final battle between Buck and Spitz?
    Spitz took a short-cut and killed the rabbit Buck was chasing. Buck was furious and attacked Spitz.

5. What was the outcome of the final battle between Spitz and Buck?
    Although Spitz at first appeared to be able to win, Buck's perseverance and intelligence finally gave him the victory.

Part IV

1. How did Buck become lead dog?
    Because he had killed Spitz, Buck thought the honor of being lead dog should be his. He simply refused to accept any other position. Francois and Perrault gave in so they could get on with their trip.

2. Was Buck a good lead dog?
    Yes, he took exceptional pride in his work and snapped the team right into its former working attitude.

3. Why did Francois and Perrault give up the team of dogs?
    Their orders were changed, so they had to give up the dogs to new drivers.

4. In what condition were the dogs when they pulled into Dawson?
    They were in very poor condition from lack of proper rest and from a long, snowy journey.

## Part V

1. Identify Charles and Hal.
    Charles and Hal bought Buck's team and became their new owners.

2. Who was Mercedes?
    Mercedes was Charles' wife and Hal's sister.

3. Why couldn't the dogs move the sled?
    The load was too heavy and the runners were iced to the ground.

4. Describe Hal, Charles and Mercedes.
    They were ignorant about life in the north and survival in the cold, and they refused to listen to sound advice.

5. What happened to all but the five experienced dogs?
    They died of starvation.

6. How did Buck meet John Thornton?
    Buck refused to travel any further with Charles, Hal, and Mercedes, so Hal was beating him. John Thornton saw Hal beating Buck and stepped in to save him.

7. What happened to Charles, Hal, Mercedes and the sled team?
    They fell through thin ice and died.

## Part VI

1. Identify Skeet and Nig.
    Skeet and Nig are other dogs at John Thornton's camp. They are, to Buck's surprise, friendly towards him.

2. How was Buck's life with John Thornton different from his life with his other masters?
    John Thornton gives Buck tender loving care and a life more like his life in the South. Buck, in turn, responds with a great devotion to John Thornton.

3. How did Buck react to Hans and Pete?
    Buck refused to notice them until he learned that they were good friends of his master.

4. Why did Buck attack "Black" Burton?
    Buck was defending his master; "Black" Burton had hit John Thornton and had sent him sprawling. Upon seeing his master's predicament, Buck rushed to his aid.

5. How did Buck save John Thornton?
> John's boat overturned in the rapids, sending him plunging into the swirling waters. Buck saw this and rushed out to help him. Realizing both he and the animal would be lost, John Thornton sent Buck back to shore, and Buck obeyed. Hans and Pete then tied a rope to Buck, and Buck rushed back out to save his master.

6. What extraordinary feat did Buck do out of love for John?
> He broke out a sled with a thousand pound load and pulled it for a hundred yards.

Part VII

1. How much money did John Thornton win on his bet, and what did he do with it?
> He won sixteen hundred dollars, which he used to pay off debts and to finance a trip to find a gold mine.

2. To where do Buck and John travel?
> They travel deep into the wilderness where few men have gone before.

3. How does Buck respond to his trip into the wilderness?
> His instincts become sharper, and he has a longing to go into the wild alone. He takes little trips away from John, seeking the wolves by instinct.

4. How did Buck kill the moose?
> He persistently stalks it, keeps it away from the herd, never gives it a moment's rest, and finally is able to kill the weakened animal.

5. What happened to John Thornton?
> He and the members of his camp were killed by Yeehat Indians.

6. What did Buck do to the Indians who killed his master?
> He attacked and killed many of them with such ferocity that the remainder of them fled in fear.

7. With his master slain and all ties to mankind broken, what does Buck do?
> He becomes a member of the wolf tribe and responds totally to the call of the wild.

# MULTIPLE CHOICE STUDY GUIDE/QUIZ QUESTIONS - *The Call of the Wild*

Part I

1. What was Buck's life like in California?
   a. He was the dog of a mean master.
   b. No one took care of him.
   c. He had the life of a work dog.
   d. He had a leisurely life.

2. What events were taking place elsewhere which would affect Buck's life?
   a. Alaska was discovered.
   b. War broke out.
   c. People had found gold in the North.
   d. There was a bounty put on him.

3. Who was Manuel?
   a. Buck's owner
   b. Judge Miller's gardener's helper
   c. Judge Miller's son
   d. Buck's friend and "playmate"

4. What did Manuel do to Buck?
   a. He fed and cared for Buck.
   b. He beat Buck.
   c. He took Buck with him hunting for gold.
   d. He took Buck and sold him.

5. Identify "the man in the red sweater."
   a. Teaches Buck that men with clubs are to be obeyed
   b. He works for Judge Miller and sells Buck for profit.
   c. He befriends Buck on the trip north.
   d. Manuel's friend

*Call of the Wild* Multiple Choice Questions Page 2

Part II

1. What happened to Curly?
	a. He was killed by wolves.
	b. He was beaten to death by the man in the red sweater.
	c. He was attacked and killed by the other dogs.
	d. He was shot by mistake.

2. What did Buck learn from seeing Curly so swiftly killed?
	a. Dogs should obey their masters.
	b. There was no "fair play" among the dogs; kill or be killed.
	c. Pull your fair share in the traces.
	d. Don't get the rest of the team mad at you.

3. What was the command for, "Stop!"
	a. Ho
	b. Mush
	c. Yo
	d. Halt

4. Identify Spitz.
	a. He bought Buck for his sled team.
	b. He killed Curly and became Buck's enemy.
	c. He was Perrault's friend.
	d. He was the shy dog in the pack.

5. How did the dogs sleep at night?
	a. They curled up with their masters by the fire.
	b. They huddled around Spitz, like a big fur ball.
	c. Perrault & Francois put up special tents for them.
	d. They each dug holes in the snow and slept there.

6. How did Perrault honor Buck?
	a. He gave Buck his leftover dinner.
	b. He put him in the #1 slot in the traces.
	c. He carefully examined Buck's feet at the end of the day.
	d. He allowed Buck to sit by the fire.

*Call of the Wild* Multiple Choice Questions Page 3

7. How has Buck changed in Part II as compared to the way he was at the beginning of the story in Part I?
 a. He has become wise to the ways of the wild.
 b. He has become a more timid animal.
 c. He has grown more dependent on man.
 d. He has made more "friends."

8. What did the dog-driver do for Buck?
 a. Made Buck a "coat" so the whip wouldn't tear his skin
 b. Made "shoes" for Buck's feet
 c. Gave him a fresh fish he had caught
 d. Pulled Spitz off of him during a fight

*Call of the Wild* Multiple Choice Questions Page 4
Part III
1. Why did Buck and Spitz first fight?
 a. It started when Buck was helping one of the other dogs in the team fight off Spitz's attack.
 b. Buck stole Spitz's sleeping hole.
 c. Spitz didn't like the special attention Buck got from the dog-driver.
 d. Spitz stole Buck's sleeping hole.

2. What unexpected incident kept Buck and Spitz from finishing their first fight?
 a. A sudden snow squall forced them to take cover.
 b. Perrault broke up the fight.
 c. Huskies raided their camp for food.
 d. A wolf attacked Perrault.

3. What happened to the team after Buck "stood up" to Spitz?
 a. They worked together in the traces better than ever.
 b. Spitz killed many of them when they, too, tried to "stand up" to him.
 c. The team followed Buck's lead.
 d. The team no longer worked together.

4. What caused the final battle between Buck and Spitz?
 a. Spitz killed the rabbit Buck was chasing.
 b. Spitz stole Buck's dinner.
 c. Spitz stole Buck's sleeping hole.
 d. Spitz attacked Buck when he was unsuspecting.

5. What was the outcome of the final battle between Spitz and Buck?
 a. Neither dog won.
 b. Buck won.
 c. Spitz won.
 d. Perrault broke up the fight.

*Call of the Wild* Multiple Choice Questions Page 5

Part IV

1. How did Buck become lead dog?
	a. Francois & Perrault immediately made him the lead dog after he killed Spitz.
	b. He "worked his way up" over a period of several months.
	c. He refused to accept any other position.
	d. He got it by default.


2. Was Buck a good lead dog?
	a. Yes, he snapped the team right into shape.
	b. He would have been, but the team missed Spitz and wouldn't cooperate.
	c. No, he was too demanding of the team.
	d. He was just average; not great but not bad.


3. Why did Francois and Perrault give up the team of dogs?
	a. They were killed.
	b. They were offered more money for the team than they could refuse.
	c. They were tired of doing this kind of work.
	d. Their orders were changed.


4. In what condition were the dogs when they pulled into Dawson?
	a. Good
	b. Poor
	c. Very poor
	d. Excellent

*Call of the Wild* Multiple Choice Questions Page 6
Part V

1. Identify Charles and Hal.
    a. Men from the South
    b. New owners of Buck's team
    c. Friends of Perrault & Francois
    d. All of the above

2. Who was Mercedes?
    a. Hal's sister
    b. Hal's wife
    c. Charles's sister
    d. No relation

3. Why couldn't the dogs move the sled?
    a. The team was in very poor condition.
    b. The runners were iced.
    c. The load was too heavy.
    d. All of the above

4. Describe Hal, Charles, and Mercedes.
    a. Ignorant about life in he North but willing take advice
    b. Knowledgeable about life in the North
    c. Ignorant about life in the North, not willing to take advice
    d. Smart people

5. What happened to all but the five experienced dogs?
    a. They drowned.
    b. They starved.
    c. They were killed by wolves.
    d. They were sold.

6. How did Buck meet John Thornton?
    a. Hal sold Buck to John Thornton to settle a gambling debt.
    b. Mercedes sold Buck to John Thornton to "get even" with Charles.
    c. John Thornton rescued Buck from a severe beating by Hal.
    d. Buck fought on John Thornton's side when John and Hal got into a fight.

7. What happened to Charles, Hal, Mercedes, and the sled team?
    a. They fell through thin ice and died.
    b. They starved to death.
    c. An avalanche fell on them.
    d. They were never heard from again.

*Call of the Wild* Multiple Choice Questions Page 7

Part VI

1. Identify Skeet and Nig.
    a. Other dogs at Thornton camp
    b. Buck's new owners
    c. Thornton's business partners
    d. Thornton's hired men

2. How was Buck's life with John Thornton different from his life with his other masters?
    a. Buck was sent South again.
    b. Buck was more mistreated than ever and was forced to fight.
    c. Buck had to work hard, but Thornton was fairly kind.
    d. Thornton gave Buck loving care and a relatively leisurely life.

3. How did Buck react to Hans and Pete?
    a. He viciously attacked them and almost killed them.
    b. He refused to notice them until he learned they were Thornton's friends.
    c. He liked them right away and played with them often.
    d. He was jealous of them.

4. Why did Buck attack "Black" Burton?
    a. Buck was defending his master.
    b. Black Burton whipped him.
    c. Buck mercilessly attacked all strangers.
    d. Black Burton reminded him of the man in the red sweater.

5. How did Buck save John Thornton?
    a. Buck saved Thornton by attacking Black Burton.
    b. Hans and Pete tied a rope around Buck, who swam through the rapids to get Thornton.
    c. Buck dug through the snow until he found Thornton.
    d. Hans and Pete tied a rope around Buck and lowered him over the snow bank so he could reach Thornton.

6. Why did Buck break out a sled with a thousand pound load and pull it for a hundred yards?
    a. John whipped him until he did it
    b. He did it for his own pride
    c. He is afraid that if he doesn't do it, John will sell him
    d. He did it out of love for John

*Call of the Wild* Multiple Choice Questions Page 8
Part VII
1. How much money did John Thornton win on his bet, and what did he do with it?
    a. Financed a gold-hunting trip and bought a new home
    b. Paid debts and bought a new home
    c. Paid debts and financed a gold-hunting trip
    d. Paid debts and put the rest in the bank

2. To where do Buck and John travel?
    a. Deep in the wilderness where few men have gone
    b. To Dawson
    c. Back to John's first camp/home
    d. South

3. How does Buck respond to his trip into the wilderness?
    a. His instincts became sharper.
    b. He travels into the wilderness alone.
    c. He seeks the wolves by instinct.
    d. All of the above

4. How did Buck kill the moose?
    a. He persistently stalked it until it weakened.
    b. He joined up with a pack of wolves to kill the moose.
    c. He ran it off a cliff.
    d. He finished it off.

5. What happened to John Thornton?
    a. He fell through thin ice.
    b. He was killed by Indians.
    c. An avalanche killed him.
    d. He lived in the wilderness the rest of his life and saw Buck from time to time.

6. What did Buck do to the Indians who killed his master?
    a. He attacked and killed many of them and the remainder fled in fear.
    b. He stalked them until he had killed every single one.
    c. He continually stole their food supply so they would die of starvation.
    d. He upset their kayak in the freezing water and they drowned.

7. With his master slain and all ties to mankind broken, what does Buck do?
    a. He remains at John Thornton's camp.
    b. He responds totally to the call of the wild.
    c. He lives with the Indians
    d. He dies

## ANSWER KEY - MULTIPLE CHOICE STUDY/QUIZ QUESTIONS
*Call of the Wild*

| Part I | Part II | Part III | Part IV | Part V | Part VI | Part VII |
|---|---|---|---|---|---|---|
| 1. D | 1. C | 1. C | 1. C | 1. B | 1. A | 1. C |
| 2. C | 2. B | 2. C | 2. A | 2. A | 2. D | 2. A |
| 3. B | 3. A | 3. D | 3. D | 3. C | 3. B | 3. D |
| 4. D | 4. B | 4. A | 4. C | 4. C | 4. A | 4. A |
| 5. A | 5. D | 5. B |  | 5. B | 5. B | 5. B |
|  | 6. C |  |  | 6. C | 6. D | 6. A |
|  | 7. A |  |  | 7. A |  | 7. B |
|  | 8. B |  |  |  |  |  |

# PREREADING VOCABULARY WORKSHEETS

# VOCABULARY - *The Call of the Wild*

Part I: Using Prior Knowledge and Contextual Clues - Part I

Below are the sentences in which the vocabulary words appear in the text. Read the sentence. Use any clues you can find in the sentence combined with your prior knowledge, and write what you think the underlined words mean on the lines provided.

1. But Buck was neither house-dog nor kennel dog. The whole realm was his.

___

2. Among the terriers he stalked imperiously, and Toots and Ysabel he utterly ignored, for he was king-

___

3. In quick rage he sprang at the man, who met him halfway, grappled him close by the throat, and with a deft twist threw him over on his back.

___

4. ...his tongue lolling out of his mouth and his great chest panting futilely.

___

5. They only laughed and poked sticks at him, which he promptly assailed with his teeth.

___

6. In his anger he had met the first advances of the express messengers with growls, and they had retaliated by teasing him.

___

7. The club was a revelation. It was his introduction to the reign of primitive law.

___

8. Perrault was a French-Canadian, and swarthy, but Francois was a French-Canadian half breed, and twice as swarthy.

___

Vocabulary - *The Call of the Wild* Part I Continued

Part II: Determining the Meaning - Match the vocabulary words to their dictionary definitions. If there are words for which you cannot figure out the definition by contextual clues and by process of elimination, look them up in a dictionary.

___ 1. realm
___ 2. imperiously
___ 3. deft
___ 4. futilely
___ 5. assailed
___ 6. retaliated
___ 7. revelation
___ 8. swarthy

A. attacked, assaulted
B. dark complexion
C. to take revenge, reprisal
D. astonishing disclosure
E. a region
F. apt, clever
G. domineering, arrogant
H. serving no useful purpose

Vocabulary - *The Call of the Wild* Parts II - IV

Part I: Using Prior Knowledge and Contextual Clues

Below are the sentences in which the vocabulary words above appear in the text. Read the sentence. Use any clues you can find in the sentence combined with your prior knowledge, and write what you think the underlined words mean on the lines provided.

1. He had been suddenly jerked from the heart of civilization and flung into the heart of things primordial.

___

2. It is true, it was a vicarious experience, else he would not have lived to profit by it.

___

3. Billie wagged his tail appeasingly, turned to run when he saw that appeasement was of no avail.

___

4. The day had been long and arduous, and he slept soundly and comfortably.

___

5. His most conspicuous trait was an ability to scent the wind and forecast it ... in advance.

___

6. Its wild water defied the frost.

___

7. Nothing daunted him. It was because nothing daunted him that he had been chosen for government courier.

___

8. With the covert mutiny of Buck, a general insubordination sprang up and increased.

___

9. Then three or four Western bad men aspired to clean out the town.

___

10. With the last remnant of his strength he managed to stagger along behind till the train made another stop.

___

Vocabulary - *The Call of the Wild* Parts II - IV Continued

Part II: Determining the Meaning - Match the vocabulary words to their dictionary definitions.

___ 9. primordial       A. difficult, laborious
___ 10. vicarious       B. a scrap, fragment, remaining
___ 11. appease         C. to aim at high things
___ 12. arduous         D. original, earliest formed
___ 13. conspicuous     E. secret, private
___ 14. defied          F. challenged, provoked to combat
___ 15. daunted         G. experienced through someone else
___ 16. covert          H. clearly in view, distinguishable
___ 17. aspired         I. to pacify, to tranquilize
___ 18. remnant         J. discouraged, intimidated

Vocabulary - *The Call of the Wild* Parts V - VI

Part I: Using Prior Knowledge and Contextual Clues
    Below are the sentences in which the vocabulary words above appear in the text. Read the sentence. Use any clues you can find in the sentence combined with your prior knowledge, and write what you think the underlined words mean on the lines provided.

1. It advertised his callowness - a callowness sheer and unutterable.

___

2. Buck watched them apprehensively as they proceeded to take down the tent.

___

3. Mercedes looked at them imploringly, untold repugnance at sight of pain written in her pretty face.

___

4. Mercedes looked at them imploringly, untold repugnance at sight of pain written in her pretty face.

___

5. The outfit, though cut in half, was still a formidable bulk.

___

6. The Outside dogs, whose digestion had not been trained by chronic famine to make the most of little, had voracious appetites.

___

7. Mercedes, who disburdened herself of copious opinions upon that topic.

___

8. She wept and importuned Heaven with a recital of their brutality.

___

Vocabulary - *The Call of the Wild* Parts V - VI Continued

Part II: Determining the Meaning

Match the vocabulary words to their dictionary definitions. If there are words for which you cannot figure out the definition by contextual clues and by process of elimination, look them up in a dictionary.

___ 19. callowness          A. difficult to deal with
___ 20. apprehensively     B. ravenous
___ 21. imploringly          C. aversion, dislike, reluctance
___ 22. repugnance        D. beseech, pray for earnestly
___ 23. formidable         E. to urge repeatedly
___ 24. voracious          F. fearfully, suspiciously
___ 25. copious            G. immature, unsophisticated
___ 26. importuned        H. abundant

Vocabulary - *The Call of the Wild* Part VII

Part I: Using Prior Knowledge and Contextual Clues
   Below are the sentences in which the vocabulary words above appear in the text. Read the sentence. Use any clues you can find in the sentence combined with your prior knowledge, and write what you think the underlined words mean on the lines provided.

1. His <u>transient</u> masters since he had come into the Northland had bred in him a fear that no master could be permanent.

   _____

2. A "miner's meeting" called on the spot, decided that the dog had sufficient <u>provocation</u> and Buck was discharged.

   _____

3. ...being careful that it should neither strangle him nor <u>impede</u> his swimming...

   _____

4. Buck performed another <u>exploit</u> not so heroic, perhaps, but one that put his name many notches higher on the totem-pole of Alaskan fame.

   _____

5. Sometimes he pursued the call into the forest, looking for it as though it were a <u>tangible</u> thing.

   _____

6. Even so, it was a hard fight, and it aroused the last <u>latent</u> remnants of Buck's ferocity.

   _____


Part II: Determining the Meaning
   Match the vocabulary words to their dictionary definitions. If there are words for which you cannot figure out the definition by contextual clues and by process of elimination, look them up in a dictionary.

   ___ 27. transient          A. heroic act, deed of renown
   ___ 28. provocation        B. something that can be touched, actual
   ___ 29. impede             C. under the surface, hidden
   ___ 30. exploit            D. fleeting, momentary
   ___ 31. tangible           E. something that stimulates angers
   ___ 32. latent             F. to hamper, to obstruct

# ANSWER KEY - VOCABULARY
## *Call of the Wild*

| Part I | Parts II-IV | Parts V-VI | Part VII |
|---|---|---|---|
| 1. E | 9. D | 19. G | 27. D |
| 2. G | 10. G | 20. F | 28. E |
| 3. F | 11. I | 21. D | 29. F |
| 4. H | 12. A | 22. C | 30. A |
| 5. A | 13. H | 23. A | 31. B |
| 6. C | 14. F | 24. B | 32. C |
| 7. D | 15. J | 25. H | |
| 8. B | 16. E | 26. E | |
| | 17. C | | |
| | 18. B | | |

# DAILY LESSONS

# LESSON ONE

Objectives
1. To introduce the unit
2. To distribute books and other related materials
3. To heighten students' awareness of the status of wildlife in our world

Activity #1

Invite a guest speaker from your local wildlife preservation society to speak to your class about the role of wild animals in our world. If no speaker is available, I am sure your local society could recommend (or perhaps even lend you) a good film on this topic.

Spend the majority of this class period showing the film or listening to and interacting with the speaker.

Activity #2

Distribute the materials for the unit: books, study guides, reading assignment sheets, etc. Explain to students how they should use these materials.

Study Guides   Students should read the study guide questions for each reading assignment prior to beginning the reading assignment to get a feeling for what events and ideas are important in the section they are about to read. After reading the section, students will (as a class or individually) answer the questions to review the important events and ideas from that section of the book. Students should keep the study guides as study materials for the unit test.

Vocabulary   Prior to reading a reading assignment, students will do vocabulary work related to the section of the book they are about to read. Following the completion of the reading of the book, there will be a vocabulary review of all the words used in the vocabulary assignments. Students should keep their vocabulary work as study materials for the unit test.

Reading Assignment Sheet   You need to fill in the reading assignment sheet to let students know by when their reading has to be completed. You can either write the assignment sheet up on a side blackboard or bulletin board and leave it there for students to see each day, or you can "ditto" copies for each student to have. In either case, you should advise students to become very familiar with the reading assignments so they know what is expected of them.

Extra Activities Center   The Extra Activities section of this unit contains suggestions for an extra library of related books and articles in your classroom as well as crossword and word search puzzles. Make an extra activities center in your room where you will keep these materials for students to use. (Bring the books and articles in from the library and keep several copies of the puzzles on hand.) Explain to students that these materials are available for students to use when they finish reading assignments or other class work early.

Nonfiction Assignment Sheet   Explain to students that they each are to read at least one non-fiction piece from the in-class library at some time during the unit. Students will fill out a nonfiction assignment sheet after completing the reading to help you evaluate their reading experiences and to help the students think about and evaluate their own reading experiences.

Books   Each school has its own rules and regulations regarding student use of school books. Advise students of the procedures that are normal for your school.

Activity #3
Preview the study questions and have students do the vocabulary work for Part I of *The Call of the Wild*. If students do not finish this assignment during this class period, they should complete it prior to the next class meeting.

# NONFICTION ASSIGNMENT SHEET
(To be completed after reading the required nonfiction article)

Name _____ Date _____

Title of Nonfiction Read _____

Written By _____ Publication Date _____

I. Factual Summary: Write a short summary of the piece you read.

II. Vocabulary
    1. With which vocabulary words in the piece did you encounter some degree of difficulty?

    2. How did you resolve your lack of understanding with these words?

    III. Interpretation: What was the main point the author wanted you to get from reading his work?

IV. Criticism
    1. With which points of the piece did you agree or find easy to accept? Why?

    2. With which points of the piece did you disagree or find difficult to believe? Why?

V. Personal Response: What do you think about this piece? OR How does this piece influence your ideas?

# LESSON TWO

Objectives
    1. To read Part I
    2. To begin the oral reading evaluations

Activity #1
    Have students read Part I orally in class. If your students have not had an oral reading evaluation this term, this would be a good chance to do one. A form is included in this unit for your convenience.

    If students do not finish reading this assignment orally, they should complete it prior to the next class period.


# LESSON THREE

Objectives
    1. To preview the study questions and vocabulary for parts II-IV
    2. To read Parts II, III, and IV
    3. To continue the oral reading evaluations (if necessary)

Activity #1
    Preview the study questions and have students do the vocabulary work for parts II-IV of *The Call of the Wild*.

Activity #2
    Have students read Parts II, III and IV. If you are doing oral reading evaluations and need this class period to continue the evaluations, have students read orally. Otherwise, have students read silently.

    If students do not complete reading this assignment in class, they should do so prior to the next class meeting.

ORAL READING EVALUATION - *Call of the Wild*

Name _____ Class _____ Date _____

| SKILL | EXCELLENT | GOOD | AVERAGE | FAIR | POOR |
|---|---|---|---|---|---|
| Fluency | 5 | 4 | 3 | 2 | 1 |
| Clarity | 5 | 4 | 3 | 2 | 1 |
| Audibility | 5 | 4 | 3 | 2 | 1 |
| Pronunciation | 5 | 4 | 3 | 2 | 1 |
| _____ | 5 | 4 | 3 | 2 | 1 |
| _____ | 5 | 4 | 3 | 2 | 1 |

Total _____ Grade _____

Comments:

# LESSON FOUR

Objectives
1. To review the main ideas and events from parts II-IV
2. To preview the study questions Part V
4. To familiarize students with the vocabulary in Part V
5. To read Part V
6. To evaluate students' oral reading

Activity #1

Quiz - Distribute quizzes and give students about 10 minutes to complete them. (NOTE: The quizzes may be either the short answer study guides or the multiple choice version.) Have students exchange papers. Grade the quizzes as a class. Collect the papers for recording the grades. (If you used the multiple choice version as a quiz, take a few minutes to discuss the answers for the short answer version if your students are using the short answer version for their study guides.)

Activity #2

Give students about 15 minutes to preview the study questions for Part V and to do the related vocabulary work.

Activity #3

Have students read Part V orally for the remainder of the class period. Continue the oral reading evaluations. If students do not complete reading these chapters during this class period, they should do so prior to your next class meeting.

# LESSON FIVE

Objectives
1. To preview the study questions and vocabulary for Parts VI & VII
2. To complete reading *Call of the Wild*

Activity #1
    Preview the study questions and have students do the vocabulary work for parts VI and VII of *The Call of the Wild*.

Activity #2
    Have students read Parts VI and VII silently. Students should complete this assignment prior to the next class period.

Activity #3
    If students finish reading early, they should begin to formulate answers to the study questions for Parts V-VII.

## LESSON SIX

Objectives
1. To review the main ideas and events of Parts V-VII
2. To prepare students for a more detailed discussion of the book

Activity #1
Do the study questions for Parts V - VII in class together as you did the questions for Parts I-IV.

Activity #2
Assign each student one or two of the Extra Discussion Questions/Writing Assignments from this unit. Explain that each student should be prepared to lead a discussion about his or her question(s) during your next class period. Give students the remainder of this class period to formulate their answers to their assigned questions.

## LESSON SEVEN

Objectives
1. To discuss the main themes and ideas presented in the novel
2. To give students a sense of responsibility by having them each lead a portion of the class discussion
3. To give students practice public speaking

Activity
Call on each student to lead a class discussion based upon the question(s) he or she was assigned in Lesson Six. Be sure to jump in when necessary to guide the discussion and to add any important points which the students may have missed.

# EXTRA WRITING ASSIGNMENTS/DISCUSSION QUESTIONS - *The Call of the Wild*

<u>Interpretation</u>

1. List ways in which Buck was able to physically adapt to being a work dog.

2. Describe Buck's relationship with each of the people who entered his life.

3. What is the importance of the setting?

4. Explain the significance of each chapter's title.

5. From what point of view is the story written? How does that affect our attitudes as we read?

<u>Critical</u>

6. Explain the significance of the title, *The Call of the Wild*.

7. Explain how Buck changes during the course of the novel.

8. Where is the climax of the story? Explain your choice.

9. Describe the law of the club and fang. Give examples from the story depicting this law in action.

10. Why was the man in the red sweater so important to Buck's transformation from tame to wild?

11. Why was Buck's killing of the Yeehat Indians the final step in his journey from dog to wolf?

12. What are the conflicts in the story, and how are they resolved?

13. What was Judge Miller's role in the story?

14. Why was Buck's relationship with John Thornton important? List examples showing the progression of their relationship.

15. What is an allegory, and in what ways could *The Call of the Wild* be considered one?

16. What is anthropomorphism? Explain its use in *The Call of the Wild*

*Call of the Wild* Extra Discussion Questions Page 2

17. Why did Jack London "kill off" Jack Thornton?

18. Evaluate Buck's owners in terms of their competence.

Critical/Personal Response

19. Is the story of *The Call of the Wild* believable? Explain why or why not.

20. Discuss the idea of "survival of the fittest" as it relates to the novel.

21. What messages are presented to the reader of this book?

22. What does "adapt" mean? Give all the examples of it that you can find in this book.

23. This book is full of actions which evoke responses. Give at least five examples.

Personal Response

24. Buck's life changed considerably during the course of the novel. Sometimes things happen in our lives and we just have to deal with the change, pick up, and move on with life. What are some of those kinds of events that affect our lives?

25. How does civilization compare to life in the wild in this story?

26. Do people hear the call of the wild?

27. Must one discard civilization's rules to live in the wild? Why or why not?

## LESSON EIGHT

Objectives
    1. To have students consider their relationship with wild animals in our world
    2. To give students the opportunity to practice writing their personal opinions
    3. To give the teacher the opportunity to evaluate students' writing skills

Activity #1
    Distribute Writing Assignment #1 and discuss the directions in detail. Give students ample time to complete the assignment.

Activity #2
    Collect the papers for grading either at the end of this period or at the beginning of the next class period.

    Follow-up: After you have graded the papers, hand them back to the students and have them rewrite their papers taking in mind your suggestions. I suggest that you use an A-C-E grading scale for grading the revisions (A = revised well, C = revised but still has some errors, E = revision done without hardly any corrections/not done at all). This scale will speed your grading time and yet still give students some feedback for their efforts.

# WRITING ASSIGNMENT #1 - *The Call of the Wild*

## PROMPT

The theme of "survival of the fittest" runs throughout this book. The strong and quick survive; the weak and slow die. Darwin suggested that this process of natural selection is one means by which evolution takes place.

In our times, man--civilization--seems to be killing off animals at an astonishing rate by pollution and habitat destruction.

One question that arises is this: By being the dominant animals on this planet, are people simply contributing to the process of natural selection, or are we overstepping our boundaries and destroying our world? Civilizations live and act within their own laws and rules. Are there "natural laws" which we ignore?

Your assignment is to write a composition in which you give your opinion as an answer to the first question in the paragraph above. Be sure to explain your opinion in detail and support your statements with facts and examples.

## PREWRITING

One way to start is to jot down your ideas relevant to your topic. Then, on your scratch paper, pick out your three best points. Organize any other thoughts you've put down to see if they can be used as supporting examples or statements for any of your three main points. Scratch out anything that's left. Now go back and jot down any more ideas you have which will support your three ideas.

## DRAFTING

A diagram of a basic, five-paragraph essay might look like this:
¶1. Introduce essay topic
¶2. Main Idea (topic sentence) followed by examples or details supporting main idea
¶3. Main idea (topic sentence) followed by examples or details supporting main idea
¶4. Main idea (topic sentence) followed by examples or details supporting main idea
¶5. Summary/Closing

## PROMPT

When you finish the rough draft of your paper, ask a student who sits near you to read it. After reading your rough draft, he/she should tell you what he/she liked best about your work, which parts were difficult to understand, and ways in which your work could be improved. Reread your paper considering your critic's comments and make the corrections you think are necessary.

## PROOFREADING

Do a final proofreading of your paper double-checking your grammar, spelling, organization, and the clarity of your ideas.

## LESSON NINE

Objective
> To review all of the vocabulary work done in this unit

Activity

Choose one (or more) of the vocabulary review activities listed on the next page(s) and spend your class period as directed in the activity. Some of the materials for these review activities are located in the Extra Activities section of this unit.

### VOCABULARY REVIEW ACTIVITIES

1. Divide your class into two teams and have an old-fashioned spelling or definition bee.

2. Give each of your students (or students in groups of two, three, or four) a *The Call of the Wild* Vocabulary Word Search Puzzle. The person (group) to find all of the vocabulary words in the puzzle first wins.

3. Give students a *The Call of the Wild* Vocabulary Word Search Puzzle without the word list. The person or group to find the most vocabulary words in the puzzle wins.

4. Use a *The Call of the Wild* Vocabulary Crossword Puzzle. Put the puzzle onto a transparency on the overhead projector (so everyone can see it), and do the puzzle together as a class.

5. Give students a *The Call of the Wild* Vocabulary Matching Worksheet to do.

6. Divide your class into two teams. Use the *Call of the Wild* vocabulary words with their letters jumbled as a word list. Student 1 from Team A faces off against Student 1 from Team B. You write the first jumbled word on the board. The first student (1A or 1B) to unscramble the word wins the chance for his/her team to score points. If 1A wins the jumble, go to student 2A and give him/her a definition. He/she must give you the correct spelling of the vocabulary word which fits that definition. If he/she does, Team A scores a point, and you give student 3A a definition for which you expect a correctly spelled matching vocabulary word. Continue giving Team A definitions until some team member makes an incorrect response. An incorrect response sends the game back to the jumbled-word face off, this time with students 2A and 2B. Instead of repeating giving definitions to the first few students of each team, continue with the student after the one who gave the last incorrect response on the team. For example, if Team B wins the jumbled-word face-off, and student 5B gave the last incorrect answer for Team B, you would start this round of definition questions with student 6B, and so on. The team with the most points wins!

7. Have students write a story in which they correctly use as many vocabulary words as possible. Have students read their compositions orally! Post the most original compositions on your bulletin board.

## LESSON TEN

Objectives
1. To give students the opportunity to practice their research skills
2. To heighten students' awareness of the fact that many species of our wild animals are vanishing
3. To give students the opportunity to fulfill their nonfiction reading assignments

Activity #1
Take your class to your school's library. Once there, distribute the Research Project Assignment and discuss the directions in detail.

Activity #2
Give students ample time to find the information they need.


## LESSON ELEVEN

Objectives
1. To give students time to work on their research projects
2. To have students practice taking information from their reading notes and putting it into a written report
3. To give the teacher the opportunity to evaluate students' writing skills

Activity
Give students this class period to work on their research projects. During this period, they should be starting their written reports. Be sure to tell students by when you expect their written reports to be completed. (You might find that your class needs a few extra days to get their written work done. They can still give an oral report in the next class period to tell the class what information they have found to date.)

# RESEARCH PROJECT ASSIGNMENT
## (WRITING ASSIGNMENT #2)
*Call of the Wild*

PROMPT

As we have discussed, *The Call of the Wild* is a story of Buck's answering the call of the wild, his transference from the world of civilization to the world of the wild.

In this project, we are going to concentrate on the world of the wild. In our times, "civilization" is spreading and taking over the habitat of many wild animals. Whether or not civilization is advancing and improving our planet or is ruining it is a question open for debate. The fact remains, however, that certain animals are running out of living space and are definitely being affected by our expanding civilization.

Your assignment is to research one of the animals on the endangered species list. Find out where and how it lives, what problems civilization is causing for it, and what, if anything, people can do to help this kind of animal if they want to.

PREWRITING

Begin by gathering information--reading books and articles about your animal. Jot down notes to help you remember the information you read.

DRAFTING

Then, go over your notes and organize them in a logical series of thoughts. (One way is to begin with basic background information about the animal, then give its current status, followed by recommendations of steps that could be taken to help it in the future.) When your thoughts are organized, begin writing your paper. Keep in mind, also, that you will give an oral report to the class to share the information you have found.

PROMPT

When you finish the rough draft of your paper, ask a student who sits near you to read it. After reading your rough draft, he/she should tell you what he/she liked best about your work, which parts were difficult to understand, and ways in which your work could be improved. Reread your paper considering your critic's comments and make the corrections you think are necessary.

PROOFREADING

Do a final proofreading of your paper double-checking your grammar, spelling, organization, and the clarity of your ideas.

## LESSON TWELVE

### Objectives
1. To have students practice public speaking
2. To enrich students' understanding of wildlife in our world

### Activity
Have students each give an oral presentation in which they share with the class the information they have found about their animals. The criteria by which this activity is done will depend upon your own students' abilities. I recommend that they should stand in front of the class with no more than a 3 X 5 card of notes from which to work. I think it is important to make students think about the information they have read rather than just having them read a report to the class. If they have to think of something to say while standing in front of the class, their brains will have to work harder. Your students may need to work from more than a few notes. Use your own best judgement. If you wish to give an evaluation of the oral reports, a form is included with this packet for your convenience.


## LESSON THIRTEEN

### Objectives
1. To prepare students for the group activity which will follow
2. To give students a break from the ordinary read-question-answer routine
3. To instruct students in basic camping and survival skills

### Activity
Invite a local Boy Scout (or Girl Scout) leader to come to your classroom and discuss camping and survival techniques. He (or she) should be sure to include information about basic equipment and skills, some "tricks of the trade" students might find useful on a camping trip, and pointers as to how to plan a camping trip.

## ORAL REPORT EVALUATION - *Call of the Wild*

Name _____  Topic _____

Class _____  Date _____  Grade _____

| SKILL | EXCELLENT | GOOD | AVERAGE | FAIR | POOR |
|---|---|---|---|---|---|
| Posture | 5 | 4 | 3 | 2 | 1 |
| Clarity of Content | 5 | 4 | 3 | 2 | 1 |
| Audibility | 5 | 4 | 3 | 2 | 1 |
| Eye Contact | 5 | 4 | 3 | 2 | 1 |
| Enthusiasm | 5 | 4 | 3 | 2 | 1 |
| _____ | 5 | 4 | 3 | 2 | 1 |

Total _____

Strengths:

Weaknesses:

Comments:

# LESSONS FOURTEEN AND FIFTEEN

<u>Objectives</u>
1. To have students actually plan a camping trip
2. To have students practice their skills of organizing and thinking logically

<u>Activity #1</u>
Divide your class into small groups of four to five students each. Explain that each group is to plan a camping trip, complete with all the details. A worksheet is provided to help students make their plans.

Give students the remainder of the class period to work on their plans.

NOTE: Visit your local AAA club or travel bureau to get maps and information about places to camp and things to do near the campsites chosen. This will help students make their trips more interesting and more accurate.

<u>Activity #2</u>
While students are working in their groups, call individual students to your desk or other semi-private area to have a conference about their first writing assignments. Give students their first papers back with your corrections noted and discuss ways in which their writing was successful as well as ways in which it could be improved. A Writing Evaluation form is included with this unit for your convenience if you choose to use it.

# WORKSHEET - Camping Trip

1. Who is going?

2. How much money do you have to spend on this trip?
    Make a budget showing how much you will need to spend and for what.

3. When are you going?
    How long will you be gone? (minimum of 3 days and 2 nights required)

4. Where are you going?
    Will you stay in one place or travel during your trip?

5. What could the weather be like?

6. What equipment will you need?
    Who will bring the equipment, and where will they get it?

7. What personal gear will each person need to bring (clothing, toiletries, etc.)

8. How will you get to where you are going?

9. What provisions should you make for eating and drinking?

10. What will you do during each day of your trip?

11. What kinds of emergencies could occur, and how will you be equipped to deal with them?

12. Are there any special requirements that need to be considered for your trip?

13. Do you need anything from anyone other than yourselves? What arrangements must be made with the other people involved?
    What will you do if those other people do not do what they say they will do?

14. Is there anything else you can think of that you may have overlooked?

WRITING EVALUATION FORM - *The Call of the Wild*

Name _____ Date _____

Writing Assignment #1 for the *Call of the Wild* unit Grade _____

Circle One For Each Item:

| | | |
|---|---|---|
| Grammar: | correct | errors noted on paper |
| Spelling: | correct | errors noted on paper |
| Punctuation: | correct | errors noted on paper |
| Legibility: | excellent | good   fair   poor |
| Communication of Idea: | excellent | good   fair   poor |

Strengths:

Weaknesses:

Comments/Suggestions:

# LESSON SIXTEEN

Objectives
1. To give students the opportunity to practice writing to persuade
2. To give the teacher a chance to evaluate students' individual writing
3. To give students the opportunity to correct their writing errors and produce an error-free paper

NOTE: Prior to this lesson, save (and/or have friends, relatives or students save) requests for contributions to charitable causes that come in the mail (to use as samples for Writing Assignment #3).

Activity #1
Distribute Writing Assignment #3. Take out several samples of requests that have actually come through the mail. Discuss the components of each solicitation so students can get some ideas about the kinds of things that are normally included.

Discuss the directions to Writing Assignment #3 orally in detail. Allow the remaining class time for students to complete the activity.

Follow-Up: Follow up as in Writing Assignment 1, allowing students to correct their errors and turn in the revision for credit. A good time for your next writing conferences would be the day following the unit test.

# WRITING ASSIGNMENT #3 - *Call of the Wild*

## PROMPT
You work in an advertising agency. You have been hired by the National Wildlife Foundation to create something they can mail to people to persuade them to make a financial contribution to the Foundation. Your assignment is to create a sample of your proposed mail-out which you would submit to the Foundation for approval.

## PREWRITING
Stop and think about what kinds of things you might include in your mailing. Make a list. Brochures? Pictures? A letter? A free gift? Stamps?

Make a list of the best reasons why someone should contribute to the Foundation.

Make a list of the possible reasons why someone wouldn't contribute to the Foundation.

Make a list of ways to overcome the reasons why someone wouldn't contribute to the Foundation.

Then, think (and make notes) about the most effective ways to convince your audience to contribute.

## DRAFTING
If your mail-out will have several different items in it, decide which item(s) will be your main sales tool (best persuader). Decide which other items you want to include

## PROMPT
When you finish the rough draft of your paper, ask a student who sits near you to read it. After reading your rough draft, he/she should tell you what he/she liked best about your work, which parts were difficult to understand, and ways in which your work could be improved. Reread your paper considering your critic's comments and make the corrections you think are necessary.

## PROOFREADING
Do a final proofreading of your paper double-checking your grammar, spelling, organization, and the clarity of your ideas.

## LESSON SEVENTEEN

Objective
    To review the main ideas presented in *The Call of the Wild*

Activity #1
    Choose one of the review games/activities included in this unit and spend your class period as outlined there. Some materials for these activities are located in the Extra Activities section of this unit.

Activity #2
    Remind students that the Unit Test will be in the next class meeting. Stress the review of the Study Guides and their class notes as a last-minute, brush-up review for homework.

# REVIEW GAMES/ACTIVITIES - *The Call of the Wild*

1. Ask the class to make up a unit test for *The Call of the Wild*. The test should have 4 sections: matching, true/false, short answer, and essay. Students may use 1/2 period to make the test and then swap papers and use the other 1/2 class period to take a test a classmate has devised. (open book) You may want to use the unit test included in this packet or take questions from the students' unit tests to formulate your own test.

2. Take 1/2 period for students to make up true and false questions (including the answers). Collect the papers and divide the class into two teams. Draw a big tic-tac-toe board on the chalk board. Make one team X and one team O. Ask questions to each side, giving each student one turn. If the question is answered correctly, that students' team's letter (X or O) is placed in the box. If the answer is incorrect, no mark is placed in the box. The object is to get three marks in a row like tic-tac-toe. You may want to keep track of the number of games won for each team.

3. Take 1/2 period for students to make up questions (true/false and short answer). Collect the questions. Divide the class into two teams. You'll alternate asking questions to individual members of teams A & B (like in a spelling bee). The question keeps going from A to B until it is correctly answered, then a new question is asked. A correct answer does not allow the team to get another question. Correct answers are +2 points; incorrect answers are -1 point.

4. Have students pair up and quiz each other from their study guides and class notes.

5. Give students a *The Call of the Wild* crossword puzzle to complete.

6. Divide your class into two teams. Use the *Call of the Wild* crossword words with their letters jumbled as a word list. Student 1 from Team A faces off against Student 1 from Team B. You write the first jumbled word on the board. The first student (1A or 1B) to unscramble the word wins the chance for his/her team to score points. If 1A wins the jumble, go to student 2A and give him/her a clue. He/she must give you the correct word which matches that clue. If he/she does, Team A scores a point, and you give student 3A a clue for which you expect another correct response. Continue giving Team A clues until some team member makes an incorrect response. An incorrect response sends the game back to the jumbled-word face off, this time with students 2A and 2B. Instead of repeating giving clues to the first few students of each team, continue with the student after the one who gave the last incorrect response on the team. For example, if Team B wins the jumbled-word face-off, and student 5B gave the last incorrect answer for Team B, you would start this round of clue questions with student 6B, and so on. The team with the most points wins!

# UNIT TESTS

# SHORT ANSWER UNIT TEST #1 - *The Call of the Wild*

I.  Matching/Identify

___ 1. Spitz                      A. John Thornton's friends

___ 2. Hans and Pete              B. Gardener who steals Buck & sells him

___ 3. Judge Miller               C. He rescues Buck from Hal

___ 4. "Black" Burton             D. Buck's owner in the Santa Clara Valley

___ 5. Man in the red sweater     E. Buck's first new masters in the North

___ 6. Charles                    F. Buck's incompetent master from the South

___ 7. Manuel                     G. They kill John Thornton

___ 8. John Thornton              H. He attacks Thornton; Buck attacks him

___ 9. Yeehats                    I. He bets Buck can't pull 1,000 pounds

___ 10. Perrault & Francois       J. He kills Curly; Buck kills him

___ 11. Curly                     K. Teaches Buck the law of the club

___ 12. Matthewson                L. Buck's friend on trip north; a Newfoundland

*Call of the Wild* Short Answer Unit Test 1 Page 2
II.  Short Answer
1. What did Buck learn from seeing Curly so swiftly killed?


2. What did the dog-driver do for Buck?


3. What happened to the team after Buck "stood up" to Spitz?


4. How did Buck become lead dog?


5. How did Buck meet John Thornton?


6. How was Buck's life with John Thornton different from his life with his other masters?


7. How did Buck save John Thornton?


8. What extraordinary feat did Buck do out of love for John?


9. How did Buck kill the moose?


10. With his master slain and all ties to mankind broken, what did Buck do?

*Call of the Wild* Short Answer Unit Test 1 Page 3

III. Essay

What is the "call of the wild," and how does Jack London use Buck to exemplify it?

IV. Vocabulary

Listen to the vocabulary words and write them down. Go back later and fill in the definitions.

1.

2.

3.

4.

5.

6.

7.

8.

9.

10.

# SHORT ANSWER UNIT TEST 2 *The Call of the Wild*

I. Matching

___ 1. Spitz

___ 2. Hans and Pete

___ 3. Judge Miller

___ 4. "Black" Burton

___ 5. Man in the red sweater

___ 6. Charles

___ 7. Manuel

___ 8. John Thornton

___ 9. Yeehats

___ 10. Perrault & Francois

___ 11. Curly

___ 12. Matthewson

A. They kill John Thornton

B. He bets Buck can't pull 1,000 pounds

C. Buck's first new masters in the North

D. He kills Curly; Buck kills him

E. He rescues Buck from Hal

F. Buck's incompetent master from the South

G. John Thornton's friends

H. Buck's owner in the Santa Clara Valley

I. Gardener who steals Buck & sells him

J. He attacks Thornton; Buck attacks him

K. Teaches Buck the law of the club

L. Buck's friend on trip north, a Newfoundland

*Call of the Wild* Short Answer Unit Test 2 Page 2

II. Short Answer

1. Where did Buck live at the beginning of the story? What was his life like there?

2. How did Buck change in Part II as compared to the way he was at the beginning of the story in Part I?

3. What caused the final battle between Buck and Spitz?

4. Was Buck a good lead dog?

5. How did Buck meet John Thornton?

*Call of the Wild* Short Answer Unit Test 2 Page 3

6. Why did Buck attack "Black" Burton?

7. How did Buck respond to his trip into the wilderness with John Thornton?

8. What happened to John Thornton?

9. With his master slain and all ties to mankind broken, what did Buck do?

*Call of the Wild* Short Answer Unit Test 2 Page 4

III. Composition

    Choose a different title for *The Call of the Wild* and explain how your title is appropriate, considering the themes and ideas presented in the novel.

IV. Vocabulary

    Listen to the vocabulary words and write them down. Go back later and fill in the definitions.

1.

2.

3.

4.

5.

6.

7.

8.

9.

10.

# KEY: SHORT ANSWER UNIT TESTS - *The Call of the Wild*

The short answer questions are taken directly from the study guides.
If you need to look up the answers, you will find them in the study guide section.

Answers to the composition questions will vary depending on your
class discussions and the level of your students.

For the vocabulary section of the test, choose ten of the
words from the vocabulary lists to read orally for your students.

The answers to the matching section of the test are below.

Answers to the matching section of the Advanced Short Answer Unit Test
are the same as for Short Answer Unit Test #2.

<u>Test #1</u>
1. J
2. A
3. D
4. H
5. K
6. F
7. B
8. C
9. G
10. E
11. L
12. I

<u>Test #2</u>
1. D
2. G
3. H
4. J
5. K
6. F
7. I
8. E
9. A
10. C
11. L
12. B

# ADVANCED SHORT ANSWER UNIT TEST *The Call of the Wild*

I. Matching

___ 1. Spitz

___ 2. Hans and Pete

___ 3. Judge Miller

___ 4. "Black" Burton

___ 5. Man in the red sweater

___ 6. Charles

___ 7. Manuel

___ 8. John Thornton

___ 9. Yeehats

___ 10. Perrault & Francois

___ 11. Curly

___ 12. Matthewson

A. They kill John Thornton

B. He bets Buck can't pull 1,000 pounds

C. Buck's first new masters in the North

D. He kills Curly; Buck kills him

E. He rescues Buck from Hal

F. Buck's incompetent master from the South

G. John Thornton's friends

H. Buck's owner in the Santa Clara Valley

I. Gardener who steals Buck & sells him

J. He attacks Thornton; Buck attacks him

K. Teaches Buck the law of the club

L. Buck's friend on trip north; a Newfoundland

*Call of the Wild* Advanced Short Answer Unit Test Page 2

II. Composition
　　Write <u>complete</u> answers to each of the following questions.

1. Explain how Buck changes during the course of the novel.

2. Describe the law of the club and fang. Give examples from the story depicting this law in action.

3. Why was Buck's killing of the Yeehat Indians the final step in his journey from dog to wolf?

4. Why was Buck's relationship with John Thornton important? List examples showing the progression of their relationship.

*Call of the Wild* Advanced Short Answer Unit Test Page 3

5. What is an allegory, and in what ways could *The Call of the Wild* be considered one?

6. What is anthropomorphism? Explain its use in *The Call of the Wild*.

7. List Buck's owners and evaluate them in terms of their competence.

8. How does civilization compare to life in the wild in this story?

*Call of the Wild* Advanced Short Answer Unit Test Page 4

III. Vocabulary

Listen to the vocabulary words and write them down. Later go back and write a story using all of the vocabulary words.

# MULTIPLE CHOICE UNIT TEST 1 - *The Call of the Wild*

I. Matching

___ 1. Spitz               A. John Thornton's friends

___ 2. Hans and Pete       B. Gardener who steals Buck & sells him

___ 3. Judge Miller        C. He rescues Buck from Hal

___ 4. "Black" Burton      D. Buck's owner in the Santa Clara Valley

___ 5. Man in the red sweater   E. Buck's first new masters in the North

___ 6. Charles             F. Buck's incompetent master from the South

___ 7. Manuel              G. They kill John Thornton

___ 8. John Thornton       H. He attacks Thornton; Buck attacks him

___ 9. Yeehats             I. He bets Buck can't pull 1,000 pounds

___ 10. Perrault & Francois   J. He kills Curly; Buck kills him

___ 11. Curly              K. Teaches Buck the law of the club

___ 12. Matthewson         L. Buck's friend on trip north; a Newfoundland

*Call of the Wild* Multiple Choice Test 1 Page 2

II. Multiple Choice

1. What was Buck's life like in California?
    a. He was the dog of a mean master.
    b. No one took care of him.
    c. He had a leisurely life.
    d. He had the life of a work dog.

2. What did Buck learn from seeing Curly so swiftly killed?
    a. There was no "fair play" among the dogs; kill or be killed.
    b. Dogs should obey their masters.
    c. Pull your fair share in the traces.
    d. Don't get the rest of the team mad at you.

3. How has Buck changed in Part II as compared to the way he was at the beginning of the story in Part I?
    a. He has become a more timid animal.
    b. He has become wise to the ways of the wild.
    c. He has grown more dependent on man.
    d. He has made more "friends."

4. What happened to the team after Buck "stood up" to Spitz?
    a. They worked together in the traces better than ever.
    b. Spitz killed many of them when they, too, tried to "stand up" to him.
    c. The team followed Buck's lead.
    d. The team no longer worked together.

5. What was the outcome of the final battle between Spitz and Buck?
    a. Neither dog won.
    b. Spitz won.
    c. Buck won.
    d. Perrault broke up the fight.

6. Describe Hal, Charles and Mercedes.
    a. Ignorant about life in the North but willing take advice
    b. Knowledgeable about life in the North
    c. Smart people
    d. Ignorant about life in the North, not willing to take advice

*Call of the Wild* Multiple Choice Test 1 Page 3

7. How did Buck meet John Thornton?
    a. John Thornton rescued Buck from a severe beating by Hal.
    b. Mercedes sold Buck to John Thornton to "get even" with Charles.
    c. Hal sold Buck to John Thornton to settle a gambling debt.
    d. Buck fought on John Thornton's side when John and Hal got in a fight.

8. How was Buck's life with John Thornton different from his life with his other masters?
    a. Buck was sent South again.
    b. Thornton gave Buck loving care and a relatively leisurely life.
    c. Buck had to work hard, but Thornton was fairly kind.
    d. Buck was more mistreated than ever and was forced to fight.

9. How did Buck save John Thornton?
    a. Buck saved Thornton by attacking Black Burton.
    b. Hans and Pete tied a rope around Buck, who swam through the rapids to get Thornton.
    c. Buck dug through the snow until he found Thornton.
    d. Hans and Pete tied a rope around Buck and lowered him over the snow bank.

10. Why did Buck break out a sled with a thousand pound load and pull it for a hundred yards?
    a. John whipped him until he did it.
    b. He did it for his own pride.
    c. He did it out of love for John.
    d. He is afraid that if he doesn't do it, John will sell him.

11. How did Buck kill the moose?
    a. He persistently stalks it until it is weakened.
    b. He joined up with a pack of wolves to kill the moose.
    c. He runs it off a cliff.
    d. He finishes it off.

12. What did Buck do to the Indians who killed his master?
    a. He continually stole their food supply so they would die of starvation.
    b. He stalked them until he had killed every single one.
    c. He attacked and killed many of them and the remainder fled in fear.
    d. He upset their kayak in the freezing water and they drowned.

13. With his master slain and all ties to mankind broken, what does Buck do?
    a. He remains at John Thornton's camp.
    b. He dies.
    c. He lives with the Indians.
    d. He responds totally to the call of the wild.

*Call of the Wild* Multiple Choice Test 1 Page 4

IV. Vocabulary: Multiple choice. Write in the letter of the word that matches the definition.

___ 1. Aspired          A. To aim at high things

___ 2. Latent           B. attacked, assaulted

___ 3. Futilely         C. astonishing disclosure

___ 4. Assailed         D. aversion, dislike, reluctance

___ 5. Indispensable    E. dark complexion

___ 6. Defied           F. necessary, essential

___ 7. Repugnance       G. a region

___ 8. Appease          H. to pacify, to tranquilize

___ 9. Certitude        I. original, earliest formed

___ 10. Formidable      J. apt, clever

___ 11. Deft            K. give a concrete or actual form to

___ 12. Callowness      L. to urge repeatedly

___ 13. Swarthy         M. to take revenge

___ 14. Retaliated      N. infallible, unmistakable

___ 15. Copious         O. abundant

___ 16. Primordial      P. difficult to deal with

___ 17. Realm           Q. under the surface; hidden

___ 18. Importuned      R. challenged, provoked to combat

___ 19. Revelation      S. serving no useful purpose

___ 20. Incarnate       T. immature, unsophisticated

# MULTIPLE CHOICE UNIT TEST 2 - *The Call of the Wild*

I. Matching

___ 1. Spitz

___ 2. Hans and Pete

___ 3. Judge Miller

___ 4. "Black" Burton

___ 5. Man in the red sweater

___ 6. Charles

___ 7. Manuel

___ 8. John Thornton

___ 9. Yeehats

___ 10. Perrault & Francois

___ 11. Curly

___ 12. Matthewson

A. They kill John Thornton

B. He bets Buck can't pull 1,000 pounds

C. Buck's first new masters in the North

D. He kills Curly; Buck kills him

E. He rescues Buck from Hal

F. Buck's incompetent master from the South

G. John Thornton's friends

H. Buck's owner in the Santa Clara Valley

I. Gardener who steals Buck & sells him

J. He attacks Thornton; Buck attacks him

K. Teaches Buck the law of the club

L. Buck's friend on trip north; a Newfoundland

*Call of the Wild* Multiple Choice Test 2 Page 2
II. Multiple Choice

1. What was Buck's life like in California?
	a. He was the dog of a mean master.
	b. He had a leisurely life.
	c. He had the life of a work dog.
	d. No one took care of him.

2. What did Buck learn from seeing Curly so swiftly killed?
	a. Dogs should obey their masters.
	b. Don't get the rest of the team mad at you.
	c. Pull your fair share in the traces.
	d. There was no "fair play" among the dogs; kill or be killed.

3. How has Buck changed in Part II as compared to the way he was at the beginning of the story in Part I?
	a. He has grown more dependent on man.
	b. He has become a more timid animal.
	c. He has become wise to the ways of the wild.
	d. He has made more "friends."

4. What happened to the team after Buck "stood up" to Spitz?
	a. The team no longer worked together.
	b. Spitz killed many of them when they, too, tried to "stand up" to him.
	c. The team followed Buck's lead.
	d. They worked together in the traces better than ever.

5. What was the outcome of the final battle between Spitz and Buck?
	a. Buck won.
	b. Neither dog won.
	c. Spitz won.
	d. Perrault broke up the fight.

6. Describe Hal, Charles and Mercedes.
	a. Ignorant about life in the North but willing take advice
	b. Ignorant about life in the North, not willing to take advice
	c. Knowledgeable about life in the North
	d. Smart people

*Call of the Wild* Multiple Choice Test 2 Page 3

7. How did Buck meet John Thornton?
    a. Hal sold Buck to John Thornton to settle a gambling debt.
    b. Mercedes sold Buck to John Thornton to "get even" with Charles.
    c. Buck fought on John Thornton's side when John and Hal got in a fight.
    d. John Thornton rescued Buck from a severe beating by Hal.

8. How was Buck's life with John Thornton different from his life with his other masters?
    a. Thornton gave Buck loving care and a relatively leisurely life.
    b. Buck was more mistreated than ever and was forced to fight.
    c. Buck had to work hard, but Thornton was fairly kind.
    d. Buck was sent South again.

9. How did Buck save John Thornton?
    a. Buck saved Thornton by attacking Black Burton.
    b. Buck dug through the snow until he found Thornton.
    c. Hans and Pete tied a rope around Buck, who swam through the rapids to get Thornton.
    d. Hans and Pete tied a rope around Buck and lowered him over the snow bank.

10. Why did Buck break out a sled with a thousand pound load and pull it for a hundred yards?
    a. John whipped him until he did it.
    b. He did it out of love for John.
    c. He is afraid that if he doesn't do it, John will sell him.
    d. He did it for his own pride.

11. How did Buck kill the moose?
    a. He persistently stalks it until it is weakened.
    b. He joined up with a pack of wolves to kill the moose.
    c. He runs it off a cliff.
    d. He finishes it off.

12. What did Buck do to the Indians who killed his master?
    a. He upset their kayak in the freezing water and they drowned.
    b. He stalked them until he had killed every single one.
    c. He continually stole their food supply so they would die of starvation.
    d. He attacked and killed many of them and the remainder fled in fear.

13. With his master slain and all ties to mankind broken, what does Buck do?
    a. He remains at John Thornton's camp.
    b. He responds totally to the call of the wild.
    c. He lives with the Indians.
    d. He dies.

*Call of the Wild* Multiple Choice Test 2 Page 4

V. Vocabulary: Multiple choice. Write in the letter of the word that matches the definition.

__ 1. Deft                A. to hamper, obstruct

__ 2. Transient           B. a scrap, fragment, remaining

__ 3. Daunted             C. under the surface, hidden

__ 4. Latent              D. a region

__ 5. Remnant             E. astonishing disclosure

__ 6. Copious             F. abundant

__ 7. Incarnate           G. original, earliest formed

__ 8. Imperiously         H. difficult, laborious

__ 9. Voracious           I. to pacify, to tranquilize

__ 10. Revelation         J. domineering, arrogant

__ 11. Arduous            K. difficult to deal with

__ 12. Appease            L give a concrete or actual form to

__ 13. Certitude          M. aversion, dislike, reluctance

__ 14. Impede             N. discourage, intimidated

__ 15. Retaliated         O. dark complexion

__ 16. Repugnance         P. apt, clever

__ 17. Swarthy            Q. fleeting, momentary

__ 18. Realm              R. infallible, unmistakable

__ 19. Formidable         S. ravenous

__ 20. Primordial         T. to take revenge, reprisal

# ANSWER SHEET - *Call of the Wild*

## Multiple Choice Unit Tests

I. Matching
1. ___
2. ___
3. ___
4. ___
5. ___
6. ___
7. ___
8. ___
9. ___
10. ___
11. ___
12. ___

II. Multiple Choice
1. A B C D
2. A B C D
3. A B C D
4. A B C D
5. A B C D
6. A B C D
7. A B C D
8. A B C D
9. A B C D
10. A B C D
11. A B C D
12. A B C D
13. A B C D

III. Vocabulary
1. ___   11. ___
2. ___   12. ___
3. ___   13. ___
4. ___   14. ___
5. ___   15. ___
6. ___   16. ___
7. ___   17. ___
8. ___   18. ___
9. ___   19. ___
10. ___  20. ___

# ANSWER KEY - *Call of the Wild*
## Multiple Choice Unit Test 1

| I. Matching | II. Multiple Choice | III. Vocabulary | |
|---|---|---|---|
| 1. J | 1. C | 1. A | 11. J |
| 2. A | 2. A | 2. Q | 12. T |
| 3. D | 3. B | 3. S | 13. E |
| 4. H | 4. D | 4. B | 14. M |
| 5. K | 5. C | 5. F | 15. O |
| 6. F | 6. D | 6. R | 16. I |
| 7. B | 7. A | 7. D | 17. G |
| 8. C | 8. B | 8. H | 18. L |
| 9. G | 9. B | 9. N | 19. C |
| 10. E | 10. C | 10. P | 20. K |
| 11. L | 11. A | | |
| 12. I | 12. C | | |
| | 13. D | | |

# ANSWER KEY - *Call of the Wild*
## Multiple Choice Unit Test 2

I. Matching
1. D
2. G
3. H
4. J
5. K
6. F
7. I
8. E
9. A
10. C
11. L
12. B

II. Multiple Choice
1. B
2. D
3. C
4. A
5. A
6. B
7. D
8. A
9. C
10. B
11. A
12. D
13. B

III. Vocabulary
1. P
2. Q
3. N
4. C
5. B
6. F
7. L
8. J
9. S
10. E
11. H
12. I
13. R
14. A
15. T
16. M
17. O
18. D
19. K
20. G

# UNIT RESOURCE MATERIALS

## BULLETIN BOARD IDEAS - *The Call of the Wild*

1. Save one corner of the board for the best of students' *The Call of the Wild* writing assignments.

2. Take one of the word search puzzles from the extra activities section and with a marker copy it over in a large size on the bulletin board. Write the clue words to find to one side. Invite students prior to and after class to find the words and circle them on the bulletin board.

3. Display maps and pictures of the Alaskan wilderness.

4. Make a bulletin board about survival skills with pictures of people surviving and camping or exploring in the wild.

5. Display articles and pictures about animals being returned to the wild. Compare Buck's return to the wild by instinct to the animals you have featured on your board.

6. If you are teaching *The Call of the Wild* and *White Fang* together, display a chart on which students can write in their observations comparing and contrasting Buck and White Fang.

7. Use a story line to show Buck's transformation from being "civilized" to being "wild."

8. If you decide to explore the theories of Social Darwinism, the bulletin board could depict different ideas relating to the survival of the fittest and the power of the masses.

9. Do a bulletin board about endangered species and wildlife preservation in conjunction with the research project.

10. Do a bulletin board about careers students could have relating to the wilderness: forest ranger, game warden, naturalist, botanist, conservationist, National Park Service employee, zoologist, etc.

11. Do a bulletin board about the national parks in our country and/or ways people respond to the "call of the wild."

# EXTRA ACTIVITIES - *Call of the Wild*

One of the difficulties in teaching a novel is that all students don't read at the same speed. One student who likes to read may take the book home and finish it in a day or two. Sometimes a few students finish the in-class assignments early. The problem, then, is finding suitable extra activities for students.

The best thing I've found is to keep a little library in the classroom. For this unit on *The Call of the Wild*, you might check out from the school library other related books and articles about wolves, Arctic expeditions, travel in the north (Alaska, Canada, etc.), camping, survival skills, vacationing in the North or California, Darwinian theories, wildlife preservation, laws of civilization, or articles of criticism about Jack London's work.

Other things you may keep on hand are puzzles. We have made some relating directly to *The Call of the Wild* for you. Feel free to duplicate them.

Some students may like to draw. You might devise a contest or allow some extra-credit grade for students who draw characters or scenes from *The Call of the Wild*. Note, too, that if the students do not want to keep their drawings you may pick up some extra bulletin board materials this way. If you have a contest and you supply the prize (a CD or something like that perhaps), you could possibly make the drawing itself a non-refundable entry fee.

The pages which follow contain games, puzzles, and worksheets. The keys, when appropriate, immediately follow the puzzle or worksheet. There are two main groups of activities: one group for the unit; that is, generally relating to the *Call of the Wild* text, and another group of activities related strictly to the *Call of the Wild* vocabulary.

Directions for these games, puzzles, and worksheets are self-explanatory. The object here is to provide you with extra materials you may use in any way you choose.

## MORE ACTIVITIES - *The Call of the Wild*

1. Have students design a book cover for *The Call of the Wild* (front and back and inside flaps).

2. Have students design a bulletin board (ready to be put up; not just sketched) for *The Call of the Wild*.

3. Use some of the related topics (noted earlier for an in-class library) as topics for research, reports or written papers, or as topics for guest speakers.

4. Compile students' research projects (endangered species) into a booklet, "publish" it and either sell it as a fundraiser for a wildlife charity, donate it to your local wildlife charity to let them use it for public awareness, or distribute copies of the book as a class project to heighten community awareness.

5. Have an Alaska Day during which you learn about the state of Alaska and/or the northern wilderness in general.

6. Research and discuss careers which deal with wildlife (vet., game warden, zoologist, biologist, etc.)

7. Have students find poems or lyrics to songs which relate to *The Call of the Wild*.

8. Have students write a short allegorical story.

9. Take time to have a class discussion (or do a writing assignment) for students to talk about their own pets, and how they think their pets would react to Buck's situation.

10. Have students do a group writing assignment in which they devise a plot summary for a sequel to *Call of the Wild*.

11. Take time to visit your local park, zoo, or wildlife refuge.

12. Have students look into your local or state zoning regulations to see if there are any provisions made for preserving wildlife areas.

13. Have students develop ways in which they personally could help preserve wildlife areas.

14. Discuss your students' experiences with the "call of the wild"--wild animals or wilderness experiences such as camping vacations, etc.

**The Call of the Wild Word List**

| No. | Word | Clue/Definition |
|---|---|---|
| 1. | ALL | Not part of everyone |
| 2. | ATE | Past tense of eat |
| 3. | BASE | Camp from which one goes out |
| 4. | BURTON | Black _____; Buck killed him for hitting Thornton |
| 5. | CHARLES | Buck's ignorant owner from the south |
| 6. | CLUB | The man in the read sweater had one |
| 7. | FANG | The Law Buck learned: Club and ___ |
| 8. | COLD | Chilly; opposite of hot |
| 9. | CURLY | Spitz killed this Newfoundland |
| 10. | DIE | Opposite of live |
| 11. | DOG | Buck, for example |
| 12. | EAR | Hearing organ |
| 13. | FIGHT | Buck and Spitz did this |
| 14. | FRANCOIS | Worked with Perrault |
| 15. | GHOST | What Indians called Buck: ___ Dog |
| 16. | GOLD | Yellow metal discovered in the North |
| 17. | HAL | Mercedes's brother |
| 18. | HARNESS | It holds dogs together and to the sled |
| 19. | HEAR | listen |
| 20. | HIT | Black Burton _____ John Thornton |
| 21. | HO | Stop - Command |
| 22. | HOWL | Wolves _____ at the moon |
| 23. | ICE | Frozen water |
| 24. | JUDGE | Mr. Miller's official title |
| 25. | LOYALTY | Traits of dogs; _____ to their owners |
| 26. | MAIL | Job of the Scott half-breed: ___ Train |
| 27. | MANUEL | Gardener's helper; sold Buck |
| 28. | MERCEDES | Charles's wife |
| 29. | MILLER | Buck's California owner |
| 30. | MOOSE | Large animal Buck killed |
| 31. | MUSH | Go - Command |
| 32. | NIG | Dog at John's camp |
| 33. | OBRIEN | Thornton's friend |
| 34. | PART | Buck had to _____ with many owners; leave |
| 35. | PAWS | Dog's feet |
| 36. | PERRAULT | He worked with Francois |
| 37. | PRIDE | To take _____ in one's work |
| 38. | RED | Color of blood and weater |
| 39. | RIVER | Charles, Hal & Mercedes are killed trying to cross one |
| 40. | SLED | Thing the dogs pulled |
| 41. | SLOW | Not fast |
| 42. | SNOW | Dogs have to work hard when it is deep |
| 43. | SOLLEKS | Name means angry one |
| 44. | SOUTH | Opposite of North |
| 45. | SPITZ | Buck killed this leader-dog |
| 46. | SURVIVAL | _____ of the fittest |
| 47. | SWEATER | Man in the red _____ |
| 48. | TEAM | Dogs worked together |
| 49. | THIEF | One who steals |
| 50. | THORNTON | Buck's last mater-friend |

| No. | Word | Clue/Definition |
|---|---|---|
| 51. | TORN | Ripped |
| 52. | TURN | Go right or left |
| 53. | USE | You ___ the whip to keep order. |
| 54. | WOLF | Animal(s) Buck met in Wilderness |
| 55. | WOODS | Where John and Buck went |
| 56. | YEEHATS | Indian tribe |

ripped

# WORD SEARCH - The Call of the Wild

```
C J R R B N Y H C C W F Q Z P A G D S T
C J T G L L V L V H E A R Y M Q L Z L W
M Z T O Q F R G L A P E I D W I O L E G
O H D W R A H F C R L T V D A P Y F D G
B V O G I N S W O L F N E M N E A R O X
R N Y R G M O I E U P R A S R L D S W
I T N U X H U M U S S B A U M R T J F R
E A T Z P S S P L T T D S R D A Y K E J
N O T R U B H L W O H T U N T U S D F T
N C I E T A Z E X L O S R T W L P J I Z
R D S P L D J Q A G R L V C O T I H D E
E P T W Y F M X G R N O I K O Q T M J R
H A R N E S S O H W T W V J D Q Z E Y J
F W H I E A Z I O N O P A U S L C L M Q
R S H D H J T B S S N D L D B I R Z M Z
A T J M A K J E T C E D G G V U M L R F
N V F H T E X N R O M O S E C W A Q C T
C C S I S G M R J L L K G M O L N H W F
O S Y A G L B D C D E H Y N D T U Q Z C
I F B X G H W X H L B Z S C S F E P Q X
S C Z V N N T C L X W R T Y W R L Z K Z
C K P B F Z N O Y S R T H P R G P X X Y
F J B S H Q S M M Q M E R C E D E S K L
```

| | | | |
|---|---|---|---|
| ALL | GHOST | MILLER | SOLLEKS |
| ATE | GOLD | MOOSE | SOUTH |
| BASE | HAL | MUSH | SPITZ |
| BURTON | HARNESS | NIG | SURVIVAL |
| CHARLES | HEAR | OBRIEN | SWEATER |
| CLUB | HIT | PART | TEAM |
| COLD | HO | PAWS | THIEF |
| CURLY | HOWL | PERRAULT | THORNTON |
| DIE | ICE | PRIDE | TORN |
| DOG | JUDGE | RED | TURN |
| EAR | LOYALTY | RIVER | USE |
| FANG | MAIL | SLED | WOLF |
| FIGHT | MANUEL | SLOW | WOODS |
| FRANCOIS | MERCEDES | SNOW | YEEHATS |

## WORD SEARCH ANSWER KEY - The Call of the Wild

```
                              C                              A       S
                  T         H E A R               L         L E
              O     F       A E I V           A   I   O       D
    O H     R A       C R L T V         M     P   Y   L         G
    B O G I N S W O L F         E     S   E   A       D         O
    R R   M O I E U P R A         M   R   R     D               R
    I U   U M U S     B A         U   R   T         D         E
    E T P     S   T       R       T   A   Y         I
    N T R U B H L W O H         U         U   T     P           E
        I E   A   E   O   S       R   W   O   S     I
      D S     L       A R   N     V   O   O     E   T
    E P   W Y F M     G H   T     I J D   D     Z   C E
    H A R N E S S O H I O   N W A U   S       I   L
    F W I E A   I   S T   N L J D       R M
    R S H H T   E T C   E G G   C I U   A
    A T   A A   E   R   O S E   O W   N
    N   F T E         L       N       U
    C   I S           D       L       E
    O   S G           L         S     L
    I     H
    S   B T                   
            O              M E R C E D E S
```

| | | | |
|---|---|---|---|
| ALL | GHOST | MILLER | SOLLEKS |
| ATE | GOLD | MOOSE | SOUTH |
| BASE | HAL | MUSH | SPITZ |
| BURTON | HARNESS | NIG | SURVIVAL |
| CHARLES | HEAR | OBRIEN | SWEATER |
| CLUB | HIT | PART | TEAM |
| COLD | HO | PAWS | THIEF |
| CURLY | HOWL | PERRAULT | THORNTON |
| DIE | ICE | PRIDE | TORN |
| DOG | JUDGE | RED | TURN |
| EAR | LOYALTY | RIVER | USE |
| FANG | MAIL | SLED | WOLF |
| FIGHT | MANUEL | SLOW | WOODS |
| FRANCOIS | MERCEDES | SNOW | YEEHATS |

# CROSSWORD - The Call of the Wild

## Across

2. Buck's ignorant owner from the south
6. Job of the Scott half-breed: ___ Train
8. opposite of live
11. not part of everyone
12. Indian tribe
13. Hearing organ
14. Black Burton _____ John Thornton
15. Stop - Command
17. chilly; opposite of hot
18. Color of blood and weater
20. You _____ the whip to keep order
21. The Law Buck learned: Club and ___
23. Black _____; Buck killed him for hitting Thornton
24. Buck had to _____ with many owners; leave

## Down

1. Buck and Spitz did this
3. mercedes' brother
4. traits of dogs; _____ to their owners
5. thing the dogs pulled
6. Go - Command
7. frozen water
9. camp from which one goes out
10. Worked with Perrault
11. past tense of eat
16. Thornton's friend
17. The man in the read sweater had one
18. Charles, Hal & Mercedes are killed trying to cross one
19. Buck, for example
22. What Indians called Buck: ___ Dog

# CROSSWORD ANSWER KEY - The Call of the Wild

|   | 1 F |   | 2 C | 3 H | A | R | 4 L | E | 5 S |   |   | 6 M | A | 7 I | L |   |
|---|---|---|---|---|---|---|---|---|---|---|---|---|---|---|---|---|
| 8 D | I | E |   | A |   |   | O |   | L |   | 9 B | U |   | C |   | 10 F |
|   | G |   | 11 A | L | L |   | 12 Y | E | E | H | A | T | S | 13 E | A | R |
|   | 14 H | I | T |   |   | 17 C | A |   | D |   | S |   | 15 H | 16 O |   | A |
|   | T |   | E |   |   | C | O | L | D |   | 18 R | 19 E |   | B |   | N |
|   |   |   |   |   |   | L |   | T |   |   | I |   | O |   | R |   | C |
|   |   |   |   |   |   | U |   | Y |   |   | V |   | G |   | I |   | O |
|   |   |   |   |   |   | B |   |   | 20 U | S | E |   |   |   | E |   | I |
|   |   |   |   |   |   |   |   |   | R |   | 21 F | A | N | 22 G |   | S |
|   |   |   |   |   |   |   |   |   |   |   |   |   |   | H |   |   |
|   |   |   |   |   |   |   |   |   | 23 B | U | R | T | O | N |   |   |
|   |   |   |   |   |   |   |   |   |   |   |   |   |   | S |   |   |
|   |   |   |   |   |   |   |   |   | 24 P | A | R | T |   |   |   |   |

Across
2. Buck's ignorant owner from the south
6. Job of the Scott half-breed: ___ Train
8. opposite of live
11. not part of everyone
12. Indian tribe
13. Hearing organ
14. Black Burton _____ John Thornton
15. Stop - Command
17. chilly; opposite of hot
18. Color of blood and weater
20. You _____ the whip to keep order
21. The Law Buck learned: Club and ___
23. Black _____; Buck killed him for hitting Thornton
24. Buck had to _____ with many owners; leave

Down
1. Buck and Spitz did this
3. mercedes' brother
4. traits of dogs; _____ to their owners
5. thing the dogs pulled
6. Go - Command
7. frozen water
9. camp from which one goes out
10. Worked with Perrault
11. past tense of eat
16. Thornton's friend
17. The man in the read sweater had one
18. Charles, Hal & Mercedes are killed trying to cross one
19. Buck, for example
22. What Indians called Buck: ___ Dog

# MATCHING QUIZ/WORKSHEET 1 - *The Call of the Wild*

___ 1. SPITZ             A. Black Burton _____ John Thornton

___ 2. CLUB              B. Hearing organ

___ 3. HIT               C. Thornton's friend

___ 4. SNOW              D. Buck killed this leader-dog

___ 5. SLOW              E. The man in the red sweater had one

___ 6. CLUB AND FANG     F. Chilly; opposite of hot

___ 7. DIE               G. Not fast

___ 8. GHOST DOG         H. You _____ the whip to keep order

___ 9. SOUTH             I. Worked with Perrault

___ 10. OBRIEN           J. Opposite of live

___ 11. RED              K. Charles's wife

___ 12. MERCEDES         L. Dog at John's camp

___ 13. USE              M. Color of blood and sweater

___ 14. FRANCOIS         N. Go right or left

___ 15. EAR              O. The Law Buck learned

___ 16. TURN             P. Dogs have to work hard when it is deep

___ 17. COLD             Q. What Indians called Buck (2 words)

___ 18. SOLLEKS          R. Buck's California owner

___ 19. MILLER           S. Name means angry one

___ 20. NIG              T. Opposite of North

# KEY: MATCHING QUIZ/WORKSHEET 1 - *The Call of the Wild*

| | | |
|---|---|---|
| _D_ 1. SPITZ | | A. Black Burton _____ John Thornton |
| _E_ 2. CLUB | | B. Hearing organ |
| _A_ 3. HIT | | C. Thornton's friend |
| _P_ 4. SNOW | | D. Buck killed this leader-dog |
| _G_ 5. SLOW | | E. The man in the red sweater had one |
| _O_ 6. CLUB AND FANG | | F. Chilly; opposite of hot |
| _J_ 7. DIE | | G. Not fast |
| _Q_ 8. GHOST DOG | | H. You _____ the whip to keep order |
| _T_ 9. SOUTH | | I. Worked with Perrault |
| _C_ 10. OBRIEN | | J. Opposite of live |
| _M_ 11. RED | | K. Charles's wife |
| _K_ 12. MERCEDES | | L. Dog at John's camp |
| _H_ 13. USE | | M. Color of blood and sweater |
| _I_ 14. FRANCOIS | | N. Go right or left |
| _B_ 15. EAR | | O. The Law Buck learned |
| _N_ 16. TURN | | P. Dogs have to work hard when it is deep |
| _F_ 17. COLD | | Q. What Indians called Buck (2 words) |
| _S_ 18. SOLLEKS | | R. Buck's California owner |
| _R_ 19. MILLER | | S. Name means angry one |
| _L_ 20. NIG | | T. Opposite of North |

# MATCHING QUIZ/WORKSHEET 2 - *The Call of the Wild*

___ 1. DIE            A. Listen

___ 2. WOODS          B. Buck, for example

___ 3. OBRIEN         C. Go - Command

___ 4. BASE           D. Camp from which one goes out

___ 5. MUSH           E. Stop - Command

___ 6. HARNESS        F. Thornton's friend

___ 7. MATTHEWSON     G. Yellow metal discovered in the North

___ 8. BURTON         H. Ripped

___ 9. SLED           I. Indian tribe

___ 10. HO            J. Frozen water

___ 11. SPITZ         K. Black _____; Buck killed him for hitting Thornton

___ 12. THORNTON      L. Wolves _____ at the moon

___ 13. YEEHATS       M. He bet Buck he couldn't pull 1,000 lbs.

___ 14. GOLD          N. It holds dogs together and to the sled

___ 15. HEAR          O. Buck's last master-friend

___ 16. TORN          P. Not fast

___ 17. DOG           Q. Thing the dogs pulled

___ 18. HOWL          R. Opposite of live

___ 19. ICE           S. Buck killed this leader-dog

___ 20. SLOW          T. Where John and Buck went

# KEY: MATCHING QUIZ/WORKSHEET 2 - *The Call of the Wild*

R    1. DIE            A. Listen

T    2. WOODS      B. Buck, for example

F    3. OBRIEN      C. Go - Command

D    4. BASE         D. Camp from which one goes out

C    5. MUSH        E. Stop - Command

N    6. HARNESS    F. Thornton's friend

M    7. MATTHEWSON    G. Yellow metal discovered in the North

K    8. BURTON      H. Ripped

Q    9. SLED         I. Indian tribe

E    10. HO           J. Frozen water

S    11. SPITZ        K. Black _____; Buck killed him for hitting Thornton

O    12. THORNTON    L. Wolves _____ at the moon

I    13. YEEHATS     M. He bet Buck he couldn't pull 1,000 lbs.

G    14. GOLD        N. It holds dogs together and to the sled

A    15. HEAR        O. Buck's last master-friend

H    16. TORN        P. Not fast

B    17. DOG         Q. Thing the dogs pulled

L    18. HOWL        R. Opposite of live

J    19. ICE         S. Buck killed this leader-dog

P    20. SLOW        T. Where John and Buck went

## JUGGLE LETTER - The Call of the Wild

1. SHGTO = 1. _____
   What Indians called Buck: \_\_\_ Dog

2. SCAOIRFN = 2. _____
   Worked with Perrault

3. REHA = 3. _____
   listen

4. VALVRUSI = 4. _____
   _____ of the fittest

5. APTR = 5. _____
   Buck had to _____ with many owners; leave

6. UES = 6. _____
   You _____ the whip to keep order

7. NEORIB = 7. _____
   Thornton's friend

8. EESHAYT = 8. _____
   Indian tribe

9. OTYLYAL = 9. _____
   traits of dogs; _____ to their owners

10. RRVEI =10. _____
    Charles, Hal & Mercedes are killed trying to cross one

11. EOKSSLL =11. _____
    Name means angry one

12. UCLB =12. _____
    The man in the read sweater had one

13. HFITE =13. _____
    one who steals

14. NAFG =14. _____
    The Law Buck learned: Club and \_\_\_

15. IDPER =15. _____
    to take _____ in one's work

16. OHLW =16. _____
    Wolves _____ at the moon

17. IGTHF =17. _____
Buck and Spitz did this

18. WATERSE =18. _____
Man in the red _____

19. OOSME =19. _____
large animal Buck killed

20. NIG =20. _____
Dog at John's camp

21. ITZPS =21. _____
Buck killed this leader-dog

22. ODCL =22. _____
chilly; opposite of hot

23. LAL =23. _____
not part of everyone

24. GDO =24. _____
Buck, for example

25. NTONTOHR =25. _____
Buck's last mater-friend

26. DGLO =26. _____
Yellow metal discovered in the North

27. SEMCEDRE =27. _____
Charles's wife

28. DLES =28. _____
thing the dogs pulled

29. UMSH =29. _____
Go - Command

30. RSEALHC =30. _____
Buck's ignorant owner from the south

31. ATME =31. _____
dogs worked together

32. WOLS =32. _____
not fast

33. UALRPRTE =33. _____
He worked with Francois

# JUGGLE LETTER ANSWER KEY - The Call of the Wild

1. SHGTO = 1. GHOST
What Indians called Buck: ___ Dog

2. SCAOIRFN = 2. FRANCOIS
Worked with Perrault

3. REHA = 3. HEAR
listen

4. VALVRUSI = 4. SURVIVAL
_____ of the fittest

5. APTR = 5. PART
Buck had to _____ with many owners; leave

6. UES = 6. USE
You _____ the whip to keep order

7. NEORIB = 7. OBRIEN
Thornton's friend

8. EESHAYT = 8. YEEHATS
Indian tribe

9. OTYLYAL = 9. LOYALTY
traits of dogs; _____ to their owners

10. RRVEI =10. RIVER
Charles, Hal & Mercedes are killed trying to cross one

11. EOKSSLL =11. SOLLEKS
Name means angry one

12. UCLB =12. CLUB
The man in the read sweater had one

13. HFITE =13. THIEF
one who steals

14. NAFG =14. FANG
The Law Buck learned: Club and ___

15. IDPER =15. PRIDE
to take _____ in one's work

16. OHLW =16. HOWL
Wolves _____ at the moon

| | | |
|---|---|---|
| 17. IGTHF | | =17. FIGHT |
| | | Buck and Spitz did this |
| 18. WATERSE | | =18. SWEATER |
| | | Man in the red _____ |
| 19. OOSME | | =19. MOOSE |
| | | large animal Buck killed |
| 20. NIG | | =20. NIG |
| | | Dog at John's camp |
| 21. ITZPS | | =21. SPITZ |
| | | Buck killed this leader-dog |
| 22. ODCL | | =22. COLD |
| | | chilly; opposite of hot |
| 23. LAL | | =23. ALL |
| | | not part of everyone |
| 24. GDO | | =24. DOG |
| | | Buck, for example |
| 25. NTONTOHR | | =25. THORNTON |
| | | Buck's last mater-friend |
| 26. DGLO | | =26. GOLD |
| | | Yellow metal discovered in the North |
| 27. SEMCEDRE | | =27. MERCEDES |
| | | Charles's wife |
| 28. DLES | | =28. SLED |
| | | thing the dogs pulled |
| 29. UMSH | | =29. MUSH |
| | | Go - Command |
| 30. RSEALHC | | =30. CHARLES |
| | | Buck's ignorant owner from the south |
| 31. ATME | | =31. TEAM |
| | | dogs worked together |
| 32. WOLS | | =32. SLOW |
| | | not fast |
| 33. UALRPRTE | | =33. PERRAULT |
| | | He worked with Francois |

# VOCABULARY RESOURCE MATERIALS

# The Call of the Wild Vocabulary Word List

| No. | Word | Clue/Definition |
|---|---|---|
| 1. | APPEASE | to pacify, to tranquilize |
| 2. | APPREHENSIVELY | fearfully, suspiciously |
| 3. | ARDUOUS | difficult, laborious |
| 4. | ASPIRED | to aim at high things |
| 5. | ASSAILED | attacked, assaulted |
| 6. | CALLOWNESS | immature, unsophisticated |
| 7. | CERTITUDE | infallible, unmistakable |
| 8. | CONSPICUOUS | clearly in view, distinguishable |
| 9. | COPIOUS | abundant |
| 10. | COVERT | secret, private |
| 11. | DAUNTED | discouraged, intimidated |
| 12. | DEFIED | challenged, provoked to combat |
| 13. | DEFT | apt, clever |
| 14. | EXPLOIT | heroic act, deed of renown |
| 15. | FORMIDABLE | difficult to deal with |
| 16. | FUTILELY | serving no useful purpose |
| 17. | IMPEDE | to hamper, obstruct |
| 18. | IMPERIOUSLY | domineering, arrogant |
| 19. | IMPLORINGLY | beseech, pray for earnestly |
| 20. | IMPORTUNED | to urge repeatedly |
| 21. | INCARNATE | give a concrete or actual form to |
| 22. | INDISPENSABLE | necessary, essential |
| 23. | LATENT | under the surface, hidden |
| 24. | PALPITANT | trembling or throbbing |
| 25. | PRIMORDIAL | original, earliest formed |
| 26. | PROVOCATION | something that stimulates anger |
| 27. | REALM | a region |
| 28. | REMNANT | a scrap, fragment, remaining |
| 29. | REPUGNANCE | aversion, dislike, reluctance |
| 30. | RETALIATED | to take revenge, reprisal |
| 31. | REVELATION | astonishing disclosure |
| 32. | SWARTHY | dark complexion |
| 33. | TANGIBLE | something that can be touched, actual |
| 34. | TRANSIENT | fleeting, momentary |
| 35. | VORACIOUS | ravenous |

# VOCABURLARY WORD SEARCH - The Call of the Wild

```
I N D I S P E N S A B L E W Y T G I B L
S Y T M V Y S H N T X V G B F W F N I R
R L T R L R U T Z X Y J Q C G R D C M V
S S M G Q F O R M I D A B L E Y R A P W
U U T N T S U R D E B P X Y C Q J R O Q
O O Q R L T D C C D R P L P M T Z N R L
I I P T Q Z R N E T F G C A M H R A T F
P R O V O C A T I O N T Y L E L I T U F
O E C P K N A O Z I X R A P D G N E N P
C P T A G I L V R W T E W I D E D C E W
B M L U L P M O O V R V H T T E N P D Q
Z I P A X L L P R R G O Q A T S F M E P
H E T E S P O M E R A C L N T A T T F V
R E C Y M S X W P D G C U T M E A P I N
R T E I R J A B N Z E A I Y M P N R E V
C R R L E T S I L E D G H O W P G I D L
J A T D M P P H L J S T K X U A I M K V
V N I Q N V I V L E R S W B V S B O W N
D S T G A X R F M A D L D B R F L R K L
B I U Q N X E M W J F X F R T N E D T M
B E D Y T M D S Y Z R E V E L A T I O N
D N E C O N S P I C U O U S N C F A S V
M T A P P R E H E N S I V E L Y P L M H
```

| APPEASE | DEFT | PRIMORDIAL |
| APPREHENSIVELY | EXPLOIT | PROVOCATION |
| ARDUOUS | FORMIDABLE | REALM |
| ASPIRED | FUTILELY | REMNANT |
| ASSAILED | IMPEDE | REPUGNANCE |
| CALLOWNESS | IMPERIOUSLY | RETALIATED |
| CERTITUDE | IMPLORINGLY | REVELATION |
| CONSPICUOUS | IMPORTUNED | SWARTHY |
| COPIOUS | INCARNATE | TANGIBLE |
| COVERT | INDISPENSABLE | TRANSIENT |
| DAUNTED | LATENT | VORACIOUS |
| DEFIED | PALPITANT | |

# VOCABURLARY WORD SEARCH ANSWER KEY - The Call of the Wild

*[Word search grid puzzle answer key]*

| APPEASE | DEFT | PRIMORDIAL |
| APPREHENSIVELY | EXPLOIT | PROVOCATION |
| ARDUOUS | FORMIDABLE | REALM |
| ASPIRED | FUTILELY | REMNANT |
| ASSAILED | IMPEDE | REPUGNANCE |
| CALLOWNESS | IMPERIOUSLY | RETALIATED |
| CERTITUDE | IMPLORINGLY | REVELATION |
| CONSPICUOUS | IMPORTUNED | SWARTHY |
| COPIOUS | INCARNATE | TANGIBLE |
| COVERT | INDISPENSABLE | TRANSIENT |
| DAUNTED | LATENT | VORACIOUS |
| DEFIED | PALPITANT | |

# VOCABULARY CROSSWORD - The Call of the Wild

**Across**
1. attacked, assaulted
4. heroic act, deed of renown
6. discouraged, intimidated
7. under the surface, hidden
10. fearfully, suspiciously
11. to pacify, to tranquilize
13. something that can be touched, actual
15. challenged, provoked to combat
16. a scrap, fragment, remaining

**Down**
2. to hamper, obstruct
3. apt, clever
5. trembling or throbbing
8. infallible, unmistakable
9. secret, private
10. to aim at high things
11. difficult, laborious
12. dark complexion
14. a region

# VOCABULARY CROSSWORD ANSWER KEY - The Call of the Wild

|   |   | 1 A | S | S | 2 A | I | L | 3 D |   |   |   |   |   |   |
|---|---|---|---|---|---|---|---|---|---|---|---|---|---|---|
|   |   |   |   |   | M |   | 4 E | X | 5 P | L | O | I | T |   |
|   |   |   |   |   | P |   | F |   | A |   |   |   |   |   |
|   | 6 D | A | U | N | T | E | D |   | 7 L | A | T | E | N | T |
|   |   |   |   |   | D |   | 8 C |   | P |   |   |   |   | 9 C |
|   |   | 10 A | P | P | R | E | H | E | N | S | I | V | E | L | Y | O |
|   |   | S |   |   |   |   | E |   |   | T |   |   |   | V |
| 11 A | P | P | E | A | 12 S | E |   |   | 13 T | A | N | G | I | B | L | E |
| R |   | I |   |   | W |   |   |   | I |   | N |   |   |   | R |
| D |   | R |   |   | A |   |   |   | T |   | T |   |   |   | T |
| U |   | E |   |   | R |   |   |   | U |   |   | 14 R |   |   |   |
| O |   | D |   |   | T |   |   | 15 D | E | F | I | E | D |   |   |
| U |   |   |   |   | H |   |   | E |   |   |   | A |   |   |   |
| S |   |   |   |   | Y |   |   | E |   |   |   | L |   |   |   |
|   |   |   |   |   |   |   |   | 16 R | E | M | N | A | N | T |   |

Across
1. attacked, assaulted
4. heroic act, deed of renown
6. discouraged, intimidated
7. under the surface, hidden
10. fearfully, suspiciously
11. to pacify, to tranquilize
13. something that can be touched, actual
15. challenged, provoked to combat
16. a scrap, fragment, remaining

Down
2. to hamper, obstruct
3. apt, clever
5. trembling or throbbing
8. infallible, unmistakable
9. secret, private
10. to aim at high things
11. difficult, laborious
12. dark complexion
14. a region

## VOCABULARY WORKSHEET 1 - *The Call of the Wild*

___ 1. TANGIBLE           A. abundant

___ 2. ASPIRED            B. domineering, arrogant

___ 3. CONSPICUOUS        C. apt, clever

___ 4. IMPERIOUSLY        D. serving no useful purpose

___ 5. EXPLOIT            E. give a concrete or actual form to

___ 6. IMPLORINGLY        F. dark complexion

___ 7. REPUGNANCE         G. to aim at high things

___ 8. COPIOUS            H. clearly in view, distinguishable

___ 9. REALM              I. a scrap, fragment, remaining

___ 10. INCARNATE         J. something that can be touched, actual

___ 11. FUTILELY          K. fleeting, momentary

___ 12. SWARTHY           L. fearfully, suspiciously

___ 13. ASSAILED          M. beseech, pray for earnestly

___ 14. FORMIDABLE        N. immature, unsophisticated

___ 15. DEFT              O. difficult to deal with

___ 16. APPREHENSIVELY    P. a region

___ 17. CALLOWNESS        Q. astonishing disclosure

___ 18. REVELATION        R. aversion, dislike, reluctance

___ 19. REMNANT           S. attacked, assaulted

___ 20. TRANSIENT         T. heroic act, deed of renown

# KEY: VOCABULARY WORKSHEET 1 - *The Call of the Wild*

| | | |
|---|---|---|
| _J_ | 1. TANGIBLE | A. abundant |
| _G_ | 2. ASPIRED | B. domineering, arrogant |
| _H_ | 3. CONSPICUOUS | C. apt, clever |
| _B_ | 4. IMPERIOUSLY | D. serving no useful purpose |
| _T_ | 5. EXPLOIT | E. give a concrete or actual form to |
| _M_ | 6. IMPLORINGLY | F. dark complexion |
| _R_ | 7. REPUGNANCE | G. to aim at high things |
| _A_ | 8. COPIOUS | H. clearly in view, distinguishable |
| _P_ | 9. REALM | I. a scrap, fragment, remaining |
| _E_ | 10. INCARNATE | J. something that can be touched, actual |
| _D_ | 11. FUTILELY | K. fleeting, momentary |
| _F_ | 12. SWARTHY | L. fearfully, suspiciously |
| _S_ | 13. ASSAILED | M. beseech, pray for earnestly |
| _O_ | 14. FORMIDABLE | N. immature, unsophisticated |
| _C_ | 15. DEFT | O. difficult to deal with |
| _L_ | 16. APPREHENSIVELY | P. a region |
| _N_ | 17. CALLOWNESS | Q. astonishing disclosure |
| _Q_ | 18. REVELATION | R. aversion, dislike, reluctance |
| _I_ | 19. REMNANT | S. attacked, assaulted |
| _K_ | 20. TRANSIENT | T. heroic act, deed of renown |

# VOCABULARY WORKSHEET 2 - *The Call of the Wild*

____ 1. Abundant
    A. daunted      B. deft      C. provocation      D. copious

____ 2. Aversion, dislike, reluctance
    A. repugnance      B. callowness      C. remnant      D. imperiously

____ 3. Something that can be touched, actual
    A. tangible      B. appease      C. primordial      D. futilely

____ 4. Necessary, essential
    A. indispensable      B. provocation      C. futilely      D. deft

____ 5. Clearly in view, distinguishable
    A. formidable      B. covert      C. appease      D. conspicuous

____ 6. Apt, clever
    A. provocation      B. callowness      C. deft      D. transient

____ 7. Fearfully, suspiciously
    A. latent      B. imperiously      C. arduous      D. apprehensively

____ 8. Astonishing disclosure
    A. realm      B. revelation      C. callowness      D. certitude

____ 9. To pacify, to tranquilize
    A. copious      B. formidable      C. appease      D. certitude

____ 10. To aim at high things
    A. aspired      B. retaliated      C. formidable      D. remnant

____ 11. Beseech, pray for earnestly
    A. swarthy      B. imploringly      C. formidable      D. tangible

____ 12. Dark complexion
    A. swarthy      B. impede      C. imperiously      D. indispensable

____ 13. To take revenge, reprisal
    A. exploit      B. certitude      C. retaliated      D. tangible

____ 14. Difficult, laborious
    A. provocation      B. transient      C. arduous      D. copious

____ 15. To urge repeatedly
    A. latent      B. importune      C. covert      D. voracious

# KEY: VOCABULARY WORKSHEET 2 - *The Call of the Wild*

__D__ 1. Abundant
    A. daunted    B. deft    C. provocation    D. copious

__A__ 2. Aversion, dislike, reluctance
    A. repugnance    B. callowness    C. remnant    D. imperiously

__A__ 3. Something that can be touched, actual
    A. tangible    B. appease    C. primordial    D. futilely

__A__ 4. Necessary, essential
    A. indispensable    B. provocation    C. futilely    D. deft

__D__ 5. Clearly in view, distinguishable
    A. formidable    B. covert    C. appease    D. conspicuous

__C__ 6. Apt, clever
    A. provocation    B. callowness    C. deft    D. transient

__D__ 7. Fearfully, suspiciously
    A. latent    B. imperiously    C. arduous    D. apprehensively

__B__ 8. Astonishing disclosure
    A. realm    B. revelation    C. callowness    D. certitude

__C__ 9. To pacify, to tranquilize
    A. copious    B. formidable    C. appease    D. certitude

__A__ 10. To aim at high things
    A. aspired    B. retaliated    C. formidable    D. remnant

__B__ 11. Beseech, pray for earnestly
    A. swarthy    B. imploringly    C. formidable    D. tangible

__A__ 12. Dark complexion
    A. swarthy    B. impede    C. imperiously    D. indispensable

__C__ 13. To take revenge, reprisal
    A. exploit    B. certitude    C. retaliated    D. tangible

__C__ 14. Difficult, laborious
    A. provocation    B. transient    C. arduous    D. copious

__B__ 15. To urge repeatedly
    A. latent    B. importune    C. covert    D. voracious

# VOCABULARY JUGGLE LETTER - The Call of the Wild

1. RYATWHS = 1. _____
dark complexion

2. MDEPIE = 2. _____
to hamper, obstruct

3. RDMIPIALOR = 3. _____
original, earliest formed

4. IASNRETNT = 4. _____
fleeting, momentary

5. ETURIDCTE = 5. _____
infallible, unmistakable

6. UOUSRDA = 6. _____
difficult, laborious

7. XLTIOEP = 7. _____
heroic act, deed of renown

8. OSIVRACUO = 8. _____
ravenous

9. EMALR = 9. _____
a region

10. BIFROEDLAM =10. _____
difficult to deal with

11. ERADTTLEAI =11. _____
to take revenge, reprisal

12. TEDF =12. _____
apt, clever

13. CTOIOPAVRNO =13. _____
something that stimulates anger

14. LULFTIYE =14. _____
serving no useful purpose

15. LAWOCNELSS =15. _____
immature, unsophisticated

16. OCCPSNUSIOU =16. _____
clearly in view, distinguishable

17. IABGTNEL =17. _____
something that can be touched, actual

18. NNCPRUGEAE =18. _____
aversion, dislike, reluctance

19. SDRAIEP =19. _____
to aim at high things

20. ETTLAN =20. _____
under the surface, hidden

21. FEIDDE =21. _____
challenged, provoked to combat

22. AAILSDES =22. _____
attacked, assaulted

23. CPOIOUS =23. _____
abundant

24. PSASNEBEILNID =24. _____
necessary, essential

25. YIPROLNILMG =25. _____
beseech, pray for earnestly

26. ORSIYIEUPLM =26. _____
domineering, arrogant

27. IPTLNTAAP =27. _____
trembling or throbbing

28. EPVRSNYLEIPAEH =28. _____
fearfully, suspiciously

29. TAARNIENC =29. _____
give a concrete or actual form to

30. EINVTORLAE =30. _____
astonishing disclosure

31. RCOEVT =31. _____
secret, private

32. EAMNTRN =32. _____
a scrap, fragment, remaining

33. UTDNEDA =33. _____
discouraged, intimidated

# VOCABULARY JUGGLE LETTER ANSWER KEY - The Call of the Wild

1. RYATWHS = 1. SWARTHY
   dark complexion

2. MDEPIE = 2. IMPEDE
   to hamper, obstruct

3. RDMIPIALOR = 3. PRIMORDIAL
   original, earliest formed

4. IASNRETNT = 4. TRANSIENT
   fleeting, momentary

5. ETURIDCTE = 5. CERTITUDE
   infallible, unmistakable

6. UOUSRDA = 6. ARDUOUS
   difficult, laborious

7. XLTIOEP = 7. EXPLOIT
   heroic act, deed of renown

8. OSIVRACUO = 8. VORACIOUS
   ravenous

9. EMALR = 9. REALM
   a region

10. BIFROEDLAM =10. FORMIDABLE
    difficult to deal with

11. ERADTTLEAI =11. RETALIATED
    to take revenge, reprisal

12. TEDF =12. DEFT
    apt, clever

13. CTOIOPAVRNO =13. PROVOCATION
    something that stimulates anger

14. LULFTIYE =14. FUTILELY
    serving no useful purpose

15. LAWOCNELSS =15. CALLOWNESS
    immature, unsophisticated

16. OCCPSNUSIOU =16. CONSPICUOUS
    clearly in view, distinguishable

17. IABGTNEL =17. TANGIBLE
something that can be touched, actual

18. NNCPRUGEAE =18. REPUGNANCE
aversion, dislike, reluctance

19. SDRAIEP =19. ASPIRED
to aim at high things

20. ETTLAN =20. LATENT
under the surface, hidden

21. FEIDDE =21. DEFIED
challenged, provoked to combat

22. AAILSDES =22. ASSAILED
attacked, assaulted

23. CPOIOUS =23. COPIOUS
abundant

24. PSASNEBEILNID =24. INDISPENSABLE
necessary, essential

25. YIPROLNILMG =25. IMPLORINGLY
beseech, pray for earnestly

26. ORSIYIEUPLM =26. IMPERIOUSLY
domineering, arrogant

27. IPTLNTAAP =27. PALPITANT
trembling or throbbing

28. EPVRSNYLEIPAEH =28. APPREHENSIVELY
fearfully, suspiciously

29. TAARNIENC =29. INCARNATE
give a concrete or actual form to

30. EINVTORLAE =30. REVELATION
astonishing disclosure

31. RCOEVT =31. COVERT
secret, private

32. EAMNTRN =32. REMNANT
a scrap, fragment, remaining

33. UTDNEDA =33. DAUNTED
discouraged, intimidated

www.ingramcontent.com/pod-product-compliance
Lightning Source LLC
Chambersburg PA
CBHW051417070526

44584CB00023B/3468